CONTAINER GARDENING

FOR ALL SEASONS

Enjoy YEAR-ROUND Color with 101 Designs

Barbara Wise

COOL SPRINGS PRESS

Growing Successful Gardeners™

MINNEAPOLIS, MINNESOTA

First Published in 2012 by Cool Springs Press, an imprint of the Quayside Publishing Group, 400 North First Avenue, Suite 300, Minneapolis, MN 55401 USA.

Cool Springs Press titles are also available at discounts in bulk quantity for industrial or sales-promotional use. For details write to Special Sales Manager at Cool Springs Press, 400 North First Avenue, Suite 300, Minneapolis, MN 55401 USA.

To find out more about our books, visit us online at www.coolspringspress.com.

ISBN-13: 978-1-59186-526-1

10 9 8 7 6 5 3 4 2 1

Library of Congress Cataloging-in-Publication Data

Wise, Barbara, horticulturist
 Container gardening for all seasons : Enjoy YEAR-ROUND Color with 101 Designs / Barbara Wise.
    p. cm.
 Includes index.
 ISBN 978-1-59186-526-1 (pbk.)
 1. Container gardening. I. Title. II. Title: 101 plant recipes for year-round color.

 SB418.W57 2012
 635.9'86--dc23

                    2011035908

President/CEO: Ken Fund
Group Publisher: Bryan Trandem
Publisher: Ray Wolf
Senior Editor: Billie Brownell
Editor: Kathy Franz
Creative Director: Michele Lanci
Design Manager: Kim Winscher
Cover Photo: Corean Komarec
Production Manager: Hollie Kilroy
Illustrator: Bill Kersey
Interior photos: All photos are by Barbara Wise, except page 240, lower right, which is by Kerry Michaels

Printed in China

CONTENTS

Dedication

To Lt. Col. Steven N. Wise, USAF (Ret), who had no idea that my writing a book would mean
he would be doing so many loads of laundry, so much housework, attending so many social events
on his own because "I have to stay to finish writing this section," taking our sons to
so many doctor appointments or school activities, and being ignored for days at a time.

Honey, let's go sit on the back porch and enjoy the garden.

Acknowledgments

I would like to thank my four sons—Jonathan, Robert, Zachary, and Buck—
for all the years that they hauled soil, planters, and plants all over our landscape as I tried out
different container recipes, for the hours of watering, and for never complaining about it.
(Laughter will erupt at this moment.)

A huge thank-you to Southern Land Company, LLC, for their dedication to keeping
distinctive horticulture a high priority in their developments and for allowing me to be a part of that.

To Carol Wintzinger for her guidance and encouragement to keep seeking new ideas;
to Yelena Petruk, whose creative handiwork is seen scattered throughout this book;
to Tim Downey and Brian Sewell for making what I do in my day job possible.

To Rita Randolph, a brilliant plantswoman and container gardening artist, who taught me that
container gardening is more than just sticking plants in a pot, and to Carol Reese, a gift from the
Tennessee Extension Service to Southern gardeners, who inspired me to see beyond the ordinary in
plants—I can never thank you two ladies enough for all that you have taught me.

To Sara Bomar Davis and Sharon Kinney and the Spring Break Beach Trip Gang for looking through
hundreds of pictures to help me choose which recipes to include—thank you!

Finally, a huge thank you to Cool Springs Press, especially Billie Brownell,
for your patience and guidance as I wrote this through one crazy spring planting season,
one son's high school graduation, another son's wedding, and another son's deployment to Afghanistan.
These are not the ideal conditions for writing my first book—
thank you for sticking with me.

In Memorium

SEVERAL YEARS AGO I SAT ACROSS FROM THE FOUNDER OF COOL SPRING PRESS and I heard his story of hunting through bookstores trying to find a book that would help him learn the basics of gardening in Tennessee. Nothing—zilch, nada, zip—was out there to guide him.

Most people would find another hobby. But not Roger Waynick.

Roger started his own publishing company to bring new gardeners like himself the information they needed simply to get started.

His voice struck a chord with me, stirring memories of my own experiences helping a young mom keep her planters going all summer or helping a retired couple finally have the lush, colorful courtyard they'd been dreaming about. Roger's publishing company gave me many resources to share with these novice gardeners—resources such as Judy Lowe's book *Month-by-Month Gardening in Tennessee and Kentucky*, and Felder Rushing's book *Tough Plants for Southern Gardens*. They helped new gardeners find a little success keeps them coming back outside each spring to try something a little more challenging.

So here's one of my favorite container combos in memory and in honor of Roger Waynick, founder and president of Cool Springs Press, who passed away March 22, 2011, at age 50.

- **3 Red Pentas** (*Pentas lanceolata* 'Butterfly Red')
  This plant is a host plant of the Sphinx moth. This is a tribute to how Roger's publishing company has helped bring gardening up from the ashes of a lost art to become one of the most popular interests in our society today.

- **3 Dusty Miller** (*Senecio cineraria*)
  This is a plant known for being tough and reliable, a perfect example of the type of plant to introduce to a first-time gardener.

- **3 Evolvulus 'Blue Daze'** (*Evolvulus nuttallianus*)
  This is a plant whose name comes from the Latin word meaning to "untwist." Unraveling the mysteries of gardening was the passion behind Roger's founding of Cool Springs Press.

I know that there is so much more to who Roger Waynick was than what I knew as one of his authors. But this one part of his life left a huge impact on my life, for which I will be forever grateful.

—Barbara

What You Need to Know Before You Even Start Looking at Plants

There will be a segment of the population who hears the phrase "baby steps" and immediately falls into laughter, remembering the much-panned psychological therapy of fictitious Dr. Leo Marvin in the movie *What About Bob*. And then there will be the group of people who hear that phrase and remember hearing the advice of a grandmama or an older friend telling them, "The task may seem overwhelming, but try to accomplish a little at a time. Finding success in each baby step will help you take another." Whether the advice comes from the ramblings of a narcissist movie character or from the heart of a trusted friend, when we find that we can have success in one small area, it gives us confidence to try again—and maybe even to take a bigger step.

When I first started working in the horticulture business, one of my favorite clients was a sweet lady who would walk into a garden center wanting to find something pretty to plant at her home. She'd look around at all the options and sometimes leave in tears, overwhelmed and often empty-handed. This same lady had a post-graduate degree from an Ivy League school, taught at a university, and, with her medical degree, was often literally responsible for saving human life. But gardening and garden design seemed daunting to her.

She was willing to pay me to create the design, purchase all the plants, and handle all the planting. But as we sipped coffee in her kitchen during our first garden consultation, I came to understand that what she longed for was the joy of planting something with her own hands, creating something beautiful, and feeling the joy of growing plants at her home. What she *really* needed was a gardening project that was not overwhelming, that was contained to a small area, and that came with clear instructions and guidance so that she could experience success. She needed to take baby steps—container gardening offered her that opportunity. Does any of this sound like you?

Sea glass or other decorative stone is a lovely way to finish off or accessorize your plantings.

I love my job of planting and maintaining hundreds of containers for different clients every year. Yet as I began working with folks like this client, I realized that what I enjoy even more is helping folks learn to love to garden. There are generations of people today who have never planted a seed or maintained a garden but who now desire to embrace the plant world—but they do not know where to even begin. That's where this book will help. I've created a "recipe" approach to container garden design and installation that takes you from an empty pot to a lush, vibrant container garden that *you* create at home.

So we'll start here, at the beginning, with some achievable container gardening projects to try to help cultivate a culture of gardening, starting with you. If you are a more experienced gardener, then even better—you'll appreciate my recipe approach to container gardening too.

The options for where you can use container plantings are limitless!

Plan Before
You Plant

Before you head over to the garden center to gather all the plant material for a project, draw a simple plan for where you want your planters to be located. Over the next few days, observe how much sun and shade these locations get, noting whether the sun is morning and/or afternoon sun. Also, take note of what will be surrounding the container and ask these questions:

- Will it be backed up against a dark, colored, or light wall?

- Will there be other plants around it in the landscape with bloom colors that you want to complement?

- If you have an irrigation system, will the container block the spray from reaching any plants behind it? Could an irrigation tube for the container be adapted from the existing irrigation system?

- When adding window boxes or deck boxes on new homes, check with your builder to see if these additions could negate a warranty or present any problems to the building materials used by the builder.

Answers to these questions will determine where (or even if) you locate a container garden.

An important issue to consider, too, is how close a water source is to a planter. I've visited gardens where containers are never planted because they have no convenient water source. This also needs to be considered when installing window boxes. I absolutely love window boxes on homes—as long as they have sliding windows that can open (I do not recommend window boxes on casement windows), the boxes are at least 10 inches deep and wide, and they can be easily accessed from either inside the home or safely with a ladder.

The only container planting that I refused to create was for a window box that was under a window that did not open, and that was also over the gabled roof of a porch that led to a steeply sloping front yard. (Somebody didn't think that design through to the end product.) That's just too dangerous a location.

Finally, make sure that the area where you want to locate a container can be easily accessed for planting, watering, or even just for installing the container. I've seen folks purchase 300 pounds of beautiful planters that they wanted to site fifty yards up a steep footpath to that extra-special little nook of their garden— only to find that it would cost them three times more than the price of the containers just to have someone install it.

Remember that old adage, "Measure twice and cut once"? Well, in this case, it's plan twice and purchase once. You'll be glad later.

Full sun plants thrive in deck box containers like these that get all day sun.

THE RIGHT-SIZED
CONTAINER

Finding the right containers for outside your home is not an overwhelming task, but some factors do need to be considered in the process. The most common mistake I see is when someone wants a big display of plants but purchases a container that only holds about a gallon of soil. The container itself may be large, made of lots of heavy material, but the container design has left little room for the soil needed to sustain a healthy plant. (Drought-loving succulent plants would be excluded from this requirement.)

As you buy containers, be sure to consider whether the container is wide and deep to prevent mature plants from drying out between watering. The more soil that is available to hold water, the less you will have to keep watering. You also want to make sure that the container is deep and wide enough to hold all the plants you want to grow, with space for additional soil needed for root development, without any soil spilling over the sides. In general, you will want the soil holding area of the container to be at least about half the height of the tallest or longest plant in your container.

Above: Starting container plantings with smaller plants than those specified can help save on costs.

Left: Containers can come in all shapes and forms like this old wooden tool box holding begonias.

These pressed pulp pots are excellent inserts to use inside a more decorative container.

Group containers together for impact.

Look at the style of your home and choose containers that mimic this style. Urns provide a traditional, formal look; glazed or clay planters and fiberglass planters can range from contemporary to earthy; and cast stone containers often provide an Old World feel. Also consider *where* these containers will be placed when choosing container colors. For example, a full sun or western-facing location is not a good choice for a black cast-iron planter. Not only do you risk literally baking the roots of the plants but a hot planter would quickly dry out the soil.

Knowing the amount of sun that will hit your container during the different seasons is also a major factor in your plant choices. I have containers on my front porch that will receive zero direct sunlight during the winter but which get about five hours of midday sun during the summer. Trying to find a plant combination that I could maintain year-round would not be a good option for this location. If you plan to plant in containers throughout the winter in areas where the containers are likely to freeze, look for metal, fiberglass, stone, or reinforced concrete, which are much less likely to crack.

Be willing to look beyond the ordinary when considering containers. I love to scour antique stores (and my own basement or attic) to find interesting "planters." I've planted moss-lined antique egg baskets, wooden wine crates, old copper barrels (with holes drilled in the bottom), and old rusted pull-wagons. As long as a container has a drainage hole, the container options are vast!

Shade-loving recipes do best in morning sun or dappled light.

The Ten Commandments of Container Gardening

Okay, boys and girls, it's time to gather 'round for a lesson from the Gospel of Gardening. Put on your best overalls and finest gardening gloves, pull up your wheelbarrow to the potting shed, and sit back on your weeding stool as I present today's sermon on the "Ten Commandments of Container Gardening." These "rules" are guidelines to help you be successful container gardeners.

I. Thou shalt begin with <u>soil</u>.
Success begins with what's in your soil.

Just like Grandma used to say, "It's what's on the inside that counts," having the right type of soil for container plantings is vital to growing season-long plantings, whether they are herbs, vegetables, annuals, or perennials. You want what is often referred to as "soilless soil," a product that is a well-draining mixture of compost, vermiculite, peat moss, and water retention particles that is free of soilborne diseases and weeds. Using regular garden soil or topsoil will cause a container mix to quickly become compacted, preventing tender roots an opportunity to grow. I personally use products like Fafard Complete Container Mix, Monrovia Organics Potting Soil, or Miracle-Gro Moisture Control Container Mix, but there are *lots* of others. You'll find the one that works best for you. I refer to this type of product in the recipes as a "container mix potting soil." I also strongly recommend *filling* the entire container with soil. Giving your plants an environment where their roots can reach deeply for nutrients will keep your containers healthy longer.

II. Thou shalt let the sun guide you in everything you do.

Wherever you place your container, be aware of how much sun (or how little sun) that container will receive. Fill that container *only* with plants that like the same sun requirements. For instance, lantana is a full sun plant that needs at least 6 hours of sun to bloom well. Know the sun requirements of your plants, and don't believe everything you read on the plant tag! Full sun in Michigan (where many plant tags are printed) is much different than full sun in south Texas. When trying a new plant, talk to someone local who is knowledgeable about the sun requirements for that plant. *In this book, recipes will be noted as:*

SUN—6 or more hours of direct sunlight each day. Be aware that 6 hours of afternoon summer sun is more intense than 6 hours of morning summer sun. In this book, recipes will be coded as sun only if they can tolerate 6 hours of sun in all locations (unless specifically mentioned otherwise in the recipe's description).

PART SUN—3 to 6 hours of direct sunlight each day. It's important to note in this requirement that this is the minimum amount of sunlight needed for the plant to achieve its flowering or foliage color potential.

SHADE—less than 3 hours of sun per day. Filtered or dappled sunlight falls under this category.

III. Thou shalt not covet your neighbor's abilities.

Know your own gardening limitations; take an honest look at your time constraints or physical limitations and plant only what you can maintain. Choose low-maintenance annual plants, such as mandevilla, allamanda, begonia, duranta, caladium, or Kimberly queen ferns, for summer containers if you know you have little time for deadheading and watering. Install irrigation tubing to your containers if you know you'll be traveling or working long past watering hours.

IV. Thou shalt know who your plant's friends are.

In these recipes, plants are combined because they have similar sun requirements and watering needs. In general, plants that like full sun and dry soil need to be planted with other plants that are happy in those same cultural conditions. It is also important to understand the plant options I provide if the plants mentioned in a recipe are not available. I give you the common name of each plant (which is sometimes the same as its genus name), the Latin name of each plant (which is the botanical genus and species name that distinguishes that plant from other plants), and often I will provide a specific cultivar name (a variety within a botanical species that has been bred for certain unique qualities). If a container recipe calls for a particular plant such as coral bells (common name) *Heuchera* (genus) 'Caramel' (cultivar), then you can sometimes find a different cultivar with similar characteristics such as *Heuchera* 'Crème Brulee'. Be diligent if substituting cultivars to read about their growth habits and sun requirements because they can be different even within the same genus.

V. Thou shalt remember your container, and keep it holey.

A container without a drainage hole is a water garden. Make sure it has good drainage. Most plants do *not* like to be waterlogged and tend to die more quickly from root rot than from drying out.

VI. Thou shalt always loosen the rootball of plants before planting them in a container.

Use either your fingers or the blade of your trowel to loosen the rootball *before* you put it into the planter to ensure that the roots start to reach out into the soil rather than keep wrapping around the root system. One of my favorite tools for gardening is a hori-hori knife—a traditional Japanese gardening hand tool with a serrated edge, a sharp point, and a curved blade. Several times throughout the container recipes I will mention, "shave the rootball." This means to use the serrated edge of a hori-hori knife or the edge of a hand trowel to remove layers of soil and the fine roots around the diameter of the rootball.

VII. Thou shalt make sure to know the mature size plants will grow during a growing season.

Instant gratification is a common theme in our society, so folks often will plant way too many plants in early spring just to fill up a container, only to find that the only plant that they see in August is one cute little sweet potato vine that overtook the other plants in the containers. Carefully read the height and width potentials of your baby plants. They can become container thugs.

VIII. Thou shalt not forget to fertilize!

Annual plants are generally heavy feeders, so use both a slow-release fertilizer, which I will refer to as a general-purpose fertilizer, such as Osmocote, at planting. Then regularly feed throughout the season with fertilizers such as Colorburst, Bloombooster, Monty's Joy Juice, Daniel's Fertilizer, or Flowertone. Bloom-boosting fertilizer refers to fertilizers that are higher in phosphorus than nitrogen and potassium. For a gentle weekly fertilizer, use Authentic Haven Brand® Manure Tea, which will help to condition the soil so that plants can absorb nutrients better.

IX. Thou shalt regularly check for pests and diseases.

There are several good products for treating aphids, pests, and fungal disease such as Bayer's All Purpose Flower Care, Neem oil, and many of the Garden Safe products.

X. Thou shalt remember the words of Hortius Culturii,
"A plant without fertilizer is weak. A plant without water is dead."

Don't forget to water your plants. Use a showerhead-type nozzle, which mimics a slow steady rainfall, when you water. A harsh jet spray of water may seem like a quick way to water plants but this will blow off the top layers of soil and leave roots more exposed to the elements. It is best when watering a container to give it a good soaking so that water saturates all the soil in the container. This will encourage the plant roots to grow deeper into the planter, which will draw water during warmer or drier times. A layer of pine fines, sand, moss, or rocks on top of the soil when you are finished planting will also help hold moisture in the soil. Remember to always leave one-half to one inch of space between the top of the planter and the top of the soil so that water has a place to pool before soaking into the potting mix. If the level of potting soil is above the rim of the planter, your water could quickly run out of the container and onto the ground without soaking in deeply, and soil around the roots could be washed away.

What Do You Mean?
How to Use This Book

Containerscaping is pretty straightforward, and I use certain phrases and assumptions often. These definitions will help you understand the terminology used in this book. Check out page 21 showing how to "read" a recipe too.

Plant Size

If no size is indicated in the recipe before the plant's name, then the size that I am recommending is a 2 ½- to 4-inch-diameter pot size. This is a common pot size for transplants, which often will be found in a flat of 18 plants. (You won't have to buy them all.)

Fertilizing

Fertilizers are composed of nitrogen, phosphorus, and potassium, referred to as NPK. The differing numbers refers to each element's relative percentage. The phrase "bloom-boosting fertilizer" refers to fertilizers that are higher in phosphorus than nitrogen and potassium. Phosphorus helps a plant's root development and boosts a plant's flowering ability. Nitrogen is needed for plants to produce chlorophyll, which allows plants to grow and also helps develop their darker green color. Potassium aids in protecting plants against diseases, improving root development, and helping photosynthesis. For a gentle weekly fertilizer, I often use Authentic Haven Brand® Manure Tea, which helps condition the soil so that plants can better absorb nutrients. There are many other fertilizers you can use. A general-purpose fertilizer will have a NPK ratio in which all the ingredients are similar to or equal to one another in their percentage, such as 10:10:10.

Watering

Terminology to be aware of when reading the recipe descriptions include:

Dry to the touch—meaning when you press down gently on the top of the soil, there is no moisture that appears around your finger or is detected by touch.

The top 2 to 4 inches of soil are dry—measured by sticking your finger into the soil to see if any moisture can be felt. There are several good, low cost moisture-detecting devices that can be found in many garden centers that will accomplish this same task if you are worried about messing up your nails!

Dry soil will be a lighter color than wet soil. Just because a plant is wilting does not necessarily mean that water is needed, but if you check the soil and the soil appears and feels very dry, watering should be your first plan of action.

Adding Container Mix

In some of the recipes I state, "Loosely fill your container with potting soil." The words "loosely fill" mean pouring the soil mix into the container without packing it down, allowing room to add those 4-inch to 1-gallon-sized plants in a recipe.

Sun Needs

You'll remember this from the Ten Commandments of Container Gardening, but just to recap:

Sun is 6 or more hours of direct sunlight each day. Six hours of afternoon summer sun is more intense than 6 hours of morning summer sun. In this book, a recipe will be identified as sun only if it can tolerate 6 hours of sun in all locations (unless specifically mentioned in the recipe description).

Part sun is 3 to 6 hours of direct sunlight each day. It's important to note that this is the minimum amount of sunlight needed for the recipe plants to achieve their flowering or foliage color potential.

Shade means less than 3 hours of sun per day. Filtered or dappled sunlight falls under this category.

Deadheading

This refers to removing the faded flowers on a plant. Use pruning scissors or your fingers to cut back the blossoms to right above the set of leaves below the faded blossom (sometimes called the "spent flower"). It is best to pinch geraniums with your fingers rather than clip them with pruners.

How To Read a Recipe

SUN PREFERENCE	CONTAINER SIZE	DIFFICULTY LEVEL
Full Sun	Small	Easy

Each recipe will have a Sun Preference, Container Size, and Difficulty Level at the top.

Shopping List

- Container mix potting soil
- 1 small bag crushed volcanic rock or lava rock
- 1 echeveria (*Echeveria* 'Black Prince') **A**
- 1 stonecrop (*Sedeveria* hybrid 'Hummelii') **B**
- 1 stonecrop (*Sedum* hybrid 'Fine Gold Leaf') **C**

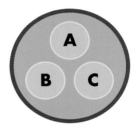

plant diagram

The shopping list will pertain to the planting diagram (above on the right) to identify each plant by its respective letter. The shopping list will also let you know if a specific cultivar is needed. If no standard size is listed in the shopping list, use the standard cell-pack size.

Each recipe has a description of how to plant, and watering and fertilizing needs. An image is included along with optional or alternate plant suggestions.

NOW WHAT?

Once the hard work is over, now what? You've observed, you've shopped, you've placed, and you've planted. Now you just need to keep your container plants alive. If you have an irrigation system going to your planters, check it often to make sure that nozzles are not clogged, that they are not getting too much or too little water due to changes in temperature, or that the clock has not been shut off due to power outages. Watering, as mentioned in the Ten Commandments of Container Gardening, is the most important aspect to maintaining your plantings so monitor your container plantings regularly. Nutrients are washed out more quickly when watering, so fertilizing the container as directed in the recipes will help keep your plantings healthy and keep flowering annuals blooming abundantly. Regularly check for pests or diseases. Don't be afraid to pinch back annual flowers by 2 or 3 inches if they start to look spindly or leggy—this actually helps them to branch out and rebloom.

There are wonderful resources available to help you as you take "baby steps" into the gardening world. Most local County Extension services are filled with helpful people full of good information to help you treat any pest or disease issues. The Extension agents and your local nurseries and home-improvement stores also can help you understand how the hardiness zone where you live may affect certain plants in your recipes or which recipes would work best in your zone. But even the best gardeners lose a few plants each year, so don't get discouraged.

Gardening is not some sort of game by which one proves his superiority over others, nor is it a marketplace for the display of elegant things that others cannot afford. It is, on the contrary, a growing work of creation, endless in its changing elements. It is not a monument or an achievement, but a sort of traveling, a kind of pilgrimage you might say, often a bit grubby and sweaty though true pilgrims do not mind that. A garden is not a picture, but a language, which is of course the major art of life.

—Henry Mitchell in *The Essential Earthman*

Getting Started

After you have gathered all your ingredients for planting your container, you should place your planter where it will be for the season. Even small containers can get heavy after adding soil, plants, and water. You can add a piece of permeable landscaping cloth, a small piece of screen material that is used in doors, or even a coffee filter over the hole in your planter if you are concerned about soil leaking out. Add enough container mix potting soil so that you have enough room in the container to put your plants and where the top of the rootballs will be about one inch below the top edge of the planter. Make sure your plants have been watered well before loosening the soil in preparation for planting. Place the plants as illustrated by the recipe diagram, adding any additional soil to fill in spaces between plants. Finish with a thin layer of pine fines, sand, small pebbles, or moss over the top of the soil. Water thoroughly to saturate all the soil—dry potting soil will quickly pull the moisture from your newly planted plants.

I also often use another trick for containers that I replant on a regular basis. I find a plastic or pressed fiber pot (which I call "inserts") that will fit comfortably within my decorative container and which allows nearly equal amounts of soil as would be in the container without the insert. Then I plant my recipe in that insert and plop it into the container, using moss to disguise any edges of the insert that may be visible until they are covered by plant growth. The advantages to this are that I can plant on a planting table instead of leaning over a container, and I can keep the mess corralled to one area. All my soil, plants, fertilizer, and tools are kept at one planting location so all I have to do is deliver the planted insert to the designated container.

Now that you know the basics of container gardening, choose a recipe and let's get started!

After 6 weeks of growth this planter is luscious.

23

S

P

R

I

N

G

Bonny Scotland

SUN PREFERENCE	CONTAINER SIZE	DIFFICULTY LEVEL
Partial Sun	Medium	Easy

Shopping List

- Container mix potting soil
- 1 1-gallon-sized Scotch broom (*Cytisus* x *praecox* 'Allgold') **A**
- 3 1-gallon-sized autumn ferns (*Dryopteris erythrosora*) **B**
- 2 1-gallon-sized coral bells (*Heuchera* 'Amethyst Mist') **C**
- 5 wintercreepers (*Euonymus fortunei* 'Coloratus') **D**
- 3 yellow violas (*Viola* x *wittrockiana*) **E**

When I first put this planter out for a client, they called and said that they were disappointed to get something that wasn't very colorful. It was very early spring and the *Cytisus* 'Allgold' looked a lot like a thick, tall, green ornamental grass. I asked them to call me back in a few weeks if they were still disappointed. Well, they did call me back but this time with praise over their vibrant planting. The Scotch broom was covered in golden flowers, the heuchera was full of light pink blooms, and the violas were blooming like crazy. New spring growth on the wintercreepers looked almost chartreuse against their purple winter color.

While Scotch broom will do fine in full sun, it will still bloom in the partial sun that the coral bells and autumn ferns flourish best in. Keep this planting evenly moist and fertilize regularly during the growing season with a general-purpose fertilizer.

Cytisus species are considered invasive in some areas so this is not a plant that I recommend planting in your landscape without first checking with your local Extension Service (to see if it's banned or otherwise not a good choice for your area). Enjoy it as an excellent container plant that can be moved to larger containers as it grows.

This spring planter combo works well as a winter planting for those in areas warmer than zone 6. Autumn ferns, coral bells, and Scotch broom are all winter evergreens in those zones.

PLANT OPTIONS

There are not many plant substitutions that will give the same effect. One of the few is to substitute pre-chilled daffodils bulbs for the Cytisus. Plant 6 to 8 daffodil bulbs about 6 inches deep. Bulbs must be pre-chilled for them to bloom during the spring. If you feel the empty space in the center of the planter looks too boring before the bulbs come up, plant a few more yellow violas where the bulbs were planted. The daffodils will come up through the violas.

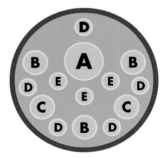

A Bright Spot

SUN PREFERENCE	CONTAINER SIZE	DIFFICULTY LEVEL
Full Sun	Medium	Easy

Shopping List

- Container mix potting soil
- 1 lemongrass (*Cymbopogon citratus*) **A**
- 1 Mexican feather grass (*Nassella tenuissima*) **B**
- 1 golden creeping jenny (*Lysimachia aurea*) **C**
- 2 purple summer snapdragons (*Angelonia*) **D**
- 1 calibrachoa (*Calibrachoa* Superbells© 'Apricot Punch') **E**
- 1 euphorbia (*Euphorbia* 'Diamond Frost') **F**
- 1 zinnia (*Zinnia* 'Zahara Fire') **G**
- 1 coleus (*Solenostemon* 'Sedona') **H**
- 1 orange nasturtium (*Nasturtium*) **I**

It's not very often that I would recommend getting *ten* different 4-inch plants and putting them all in one pot. But my friend Linda put together this planter when her garden was on a home tour and it garnered lots of attention. People *raved* about the interesting combination of textures and the pops of orange in the nasturtium, zinnia, coleus, and in the throat of the calibrachoa.

These plants need to be placed very close together to get the instant gratification look shown in this picture. An option would be to combine all ingredients in a larger-sized container than the one shown here and give them a month to fill in. If substituting cultivars, look to see if the growth patterns are similar in height and form—you don't want to substitute a trailing *Angelonia* for an upright cultivar, for example.

After planting each variety according to the recipe, gently take a few strands of the Mexican feather grass and pull them through sections of the other plants. This helps to give the blades of grass a random look of weaving its way through the planting. With this many plants in one planter, diligence in keeping everything watered is vital to the long-term beauty of the flowers. The nasturtium will be the indicator plant if these flowers are past due for a watering because it will be the first to wilt. Feed with a liquid bloom-boosting fertilizer once a month.

If you live in tropical areas such as zones 9 and 10, use this planting as a winter recipe. For those of you living in climates colder than zones 2 to 5, this recipe would be a good summertime combination.

PLANT OPTIONS

Each of the plant varieties mentioned in this recipe are common enough to find in most zones around the country but you may not be able to replicate each cultivar. Solenestemon *'Henna' or 'Alabama' would be good substitutes for 'Sedona',* and Zinnia *'Profusion Fire' could be used if 'Zahara Fire' is not available.* Gypsophila *'Snowflake' could be used instead of the* Euphorbia *and* Antirrhinum, *commonly called a cut flower snapdragon, could be used to replace the* Angelonia.

Bring It On!

Shopping List

- Container mix potting soil
- 1 1-gallon-sized ti plant (*Cordyline terminalis* 'Exotica') **A**
- 1 1-gallon-size cordyline (*Cordyline* 'Cabernett') **B**
- 5 coleus (*Solenostemon* 'Wizard Rose') **C**
- 1 summer snapdragon (*Angelonia* 'Angelmist Plum') **D**
- 1 1-quart-sized ivy (*Hedera helix* 'Glacier') **E**
- 1 1-gallon-sized coral bells (*Heuchera* 'Georgia Peach') **F**
- 2 snapdragons (*Antirrhinum majus* 'Trailing Red') **G**

This is a container recipe for those who aren't afraid of getting attention. With texture, form, and rich color coming at you from all over the container, be prepared for the neighbors to drop by on a regular basis just to see what this recipe will look like as it grows. This container recipe was first spotted in North Carolina at a garden filled with other *gorgeous* containers and landscaping, but this planting still grabbed a good share of the attention. In climates cooler than zone 5, this recipe can be placed in full sun to produce more prolific flowering in the *Angelonia* and red snapdragon.

Begin by filling your planter about three-fourths full of container mix potting soil. Position the two different *Cordyline* plants as shown in the recipe diagram, but angle them slightly away from each other. You may need to add more soil at this point to hold the plants in position and to elevate the soil for planting the remaining ingredients. Plant the coleus next, followed by the ivy and coral bells, tilting the coral bells toward the outside of the planter. Finish by planting the remaining ingredients as shown by the recipe diagram. In early spring you will see a good bit more blooms on the red snapdragon than you will on the *Angelonia*, but as the temperatures warm up, so does the summer snapdragon. The coleus will keep trying to send up lovely spikes of blue flowers, but keep pinching those back to encourage bushier growth in these plants. If you keep this planting through the summer, keep pinching the coleus until August, then allow it to explode with blooms. In warmer climates, this recipe will need to be protected from afternoon sun when carried over for the summer. Fertilize monthly with a general-purpose fertilizer. You only need to water when the top two inches of soil are dry to the touch.

PLANT OPTIONS

Trailing red carnations, Dianthus caryophyllus, *are an easy substitute for the red snapdragons. If cooler temperatures have you worried about the* Angelonia *blooming, use blue delphinium.*

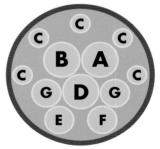

Fern-tastic Combo

SUN PREFERENCE	CONTAINER SIZE	DIFFICULTY LEVEL
Shade	Medium	Easy

Shopping List

- Container mix potting soil
- 3 gold Boston ferns (*Nephrolepis exaltata* 'Rita's Gold™') **A**
- 1 1-gallon-sized rhizomatous begonia (*Begonia* 'River Nile') **B**
- 1 coleus (*Solenostemon* 'Sultana') **C**
- 3 wishbone flowers (*Torenia* 'Summer Wave Amythest') **D**
- 1 chocolate creeping jenny (*Lysimachia congestiflora* 'Persian Chocolate') **E**

Different recipes in this book have special meanings to me for one reason or another, and this recipe has connections to one person who helped change my whole way of looking at container gardening. I first went to hear Rita Randolph of Randolph's Greenhouses (Jackson, Tennessee) during my early years of gardening; I would write *pages* of notes as she described one unique plant after another that she had growing in her greenhouse. The "plant nerd" in me organized trips to visit her nursery and Rita graciously coached me along, sharing her plant knowledge. On one of my pilgrimages to see what new plant Rita was growing, I saw the most incredible chartreuse fern, which I soon found out was a plant she had discovered. 'Rita's Gold' fern became my new favorite plant for shade and part sun containers because of the way it brightens up darker areas like a burst of sunlight.

After loosely filling your planter with container mix potting soil, leaving about 2 inches from the top of the container, center the begonia and coleus as directed by the recipe diagram. Next, plant the 'Rita's Gold' fern, slightly tilting the fern toward the outside of the planter. Finally, add your trailing *Torenia* and *Lysimachia*. Keep the coleus from flowering during the first two months in the container to encourage it to become fuller. This *Lysimachia* can grow prolifically so you might need to trim it back throughout the season. Look for the surprise pop of yellow flower from the creeping jenny at intervals during its growth.

Begonias do not like to stay wet so water this only when the top two inches of soil have dried out. The coleus or summer snapdragons are good indicator plants to help you know when to water. When they start to wilt, it's time to water. Fertilize monthly with a general-purpose fertilizer.

PLANT OPTIONS

Tiger fern, Nephrolepis exaltata, *can be substituted for 'Rita's Gold' fern, just don't tell me about it.*

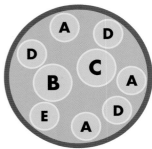

Foliage Fantasy

SUN PREFERENCE	CONTAINER SIZE	DIFFICULTY LEVEL
Partial Sun	Medium	Easy

Shopping List

- Container mix potting soil
- 1 1-gallon-sized skimmia (*Skimmia japonica*) **A**
- 1 sweet flag grass (*Acorus gramineus* 'Ogon') **B**
- 3 coral bells (*Heuchera* 'Silver Scrolls') **C**
- 2 1-quart-sized Blue Creeper® junipers (*Juniperus scopulorum* 'Monam') **D**
- 4 purple-leafed wintercreepers (*Euonymus fortunei* 'Coloratus') **E**
- 4 blue pansies (*Viola* x *wittrockiana*) **F**

Go ahead and admit it. There are some of you out there that just are not flower people. You love plants, you enjoy seeing interesting containers, but you just don't like the litter of flower petals on your porch. Or maybe you just like the often more subtle display of foliage plants. While I have snuck a few little flowers in this recipe, this combination may be just what you are looking for in a container planting. Use this low-growing combination for a tabletop planter or to fill in an empty corner of your stairway.

Use a wide, shallow container (at least 8 inches diameter) to replicate the look of this recipe. Fill it with container mix potting soil, leaving about 3 inches from the top of the planter. Center the skimmia and then add the sweet flag grass. You may need to gently spread the blades of the grass to create the look you like. Then place the *Heuchera*, giving them a slight tilt to the outside of the container. Continue planting the remaining ingredients as directed by the recipe diagram. You may need to add more soil to fill in spaces between plants.

In early spring, the skimmia will produce a white flower as will the coral bells. These produce very little "litter" for the foliage fiend, but the pansies will step up their flower production with the warming temperatures. This easy care recipe only needs to be watered when the top two inches of soil are dry to the touch. Fertilize once a month with a general-purpose fertilizer. This recipe is easy to maintain over the summer; all you have to do is replace the pansies with purple summer snapdragons.

PLANT OPTIONS

For those who want even more foliage and fewer flowers, substitute the pansies with scotch moss, Sagina subulata *'Aurea', or* Pachysandra terminalis.

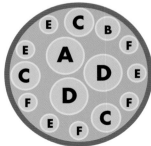

Just Here for the Party

SUN PREFERENCE	CONTAINER SIZE	DIFFICULTY LEVEL
Partial Sun	**Large**	**Easy**

Shopping List

- Container mix potting soil
- 1 3-gallon-sized bamboo (*Fargesia rufa* 'Sunset Glow') **A**
- 4 Algerian ivies (*Hedera canariensis*) **B**
- 2 1-gallon-sized coral bells (*Heuchera* 'Palace Purple') **C**
- 1 1-gallon-sized cheddar pinks (*Dianthus* 'Frosted Fire') **D**

A co-worker at my landscaping business told me this was his favorite combination. I was a little puzzled by this until he explained that this container recipe, Just Here for the Party, can be enjoyed by more than just one of the senses. There is the obvious visual enjoyment of seeing the different plant textures, the different shades of green among the bamboo, Algerian ivy, and 'Frosted Fire' cheddar pinks, and the deep pinks of the *Dianthus* flower that is repeated by the deep pink on the undersides of the 'Palace Purple'. But there is also the clove-scented fragrance of the *Dianthus* flower that comes in wafts with the wind. The wind will produce a third sensory delight with the gentle rushing sound of the bamboo on a breezy day. For being such a simple planting, this combination did prove to be a sensory party animal!

This container combination is designed to be placed where its backside cannot be seen, which involves placing the planter up against a wall or a solid hedge, so start planting by placing the bamboo along the back of the container rather than the middle of the planter. This will give the remaining plants the opportunity to spread out and show off their beauty. Plant the *Dianthus* at a slight angle facing the edge of the planter so that the foliage will spill quickly over the edge. Other cultivars of *Dianthus* can be substituted for 'Frosted Fire', such as 'Pixie Star', 'Firewitch', or 'Bath's Pink'.

This planting is designed for spring containers but in zones 6 and warmer, these plants are all evergreens and can be used as a year-round planting. Use a general-purpose fertilizer twice a year to maintain this planting. Water when the soil is dry to the touch.

PLANT OPTIONS

If you have difficulty finding Algerian ivy or bamboo, English ivy can be substituted. Bamboo may be more difficult to locate in climates colder than zone 5 and a substitute of Chasmanthium latifolium, *also called northern sea oats, or* Panicum virgatum *'Shenandoah' switch grass could be used.*

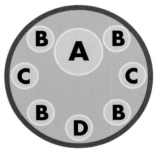

Lazy-Daisy Crazy

SUN PREFERENCE	CONTAINER SIZE	DIFFICULTY LEVEL
Partial Sun	Medium	Easy

Shopping List

- Container mix potting soil
- 3 African daisies (*Osteospermum* 'Serenity® Vanilla') **A**
- 1 sweet potato vine (*Ipomoea* 'Ace of Spades') **B**
- 3 Japanese sedges (*Carex* 'Frosted Curls') **C**
- 5 wishbone flowers (*Torenia* 'Summer Wave Large Violet') **D**

When I first saw this container design down in Florida early one spring, I was impressed by the repetition of color throughout it. The violet flowers of the *Torenia* are echoed in the violet centers of the African daisy and in the deep violet veins of the sweet potato leaves. White African daisy petals are echoed in the thin blades of the *Carex* grass and the white throats of the wishbone flower. You may also infrequently see a lavender-tinged white bloom from this sweet potato vine. *Osteospermum*, which is the African daisy, is a prolific and beautiful bloomer during the spring for those in the warmer climates but it will tend to rest from blooming when temperature remain above the upper 80s. This recipe could last through the summer for those in the milder zones of 3 to 5 if it's kept regularly fertilized.

Fill the planter with container mix potting soil, leaving about two inches of space from the top of the container. Plant the African daisy first as shown by the recipe diagram, followed by the sweet potato vine and Japanese sedges. Tilt the Japanese sedges slightly toward the outer rim of the planter to encourage a spilling effect. Finally, plant the wishbone flowers as shown. This recipe was designed to use 4-inch-sized plants because these plants all will grow quickly to fill out the container, so don't be surprised if this recipe doesn't look immediately like the picture shown here if you use smaller ones. To achieve a more instant gratification look, plant 6-inch-sized or gallon-sized potted plants in your container.

Water this recipe when the top of the soil is dry to the touch. Fertilize once a month with a bloom-boosting fertilizer. Trim off faded blooms to maintain a neat appearance in the planter. The African daisy also makes a nice cut flower to enjoy indoors.

PLANT OPTIONS

To give this recipe a wilder look, substitute 'Crazy Daisy' Shasta daisy, Leucanthemum x superbum, *for the African daisy. Blue bacopa,* Sutera cordata *'Blutopia', could be used instead of the wishbone flower.*

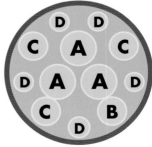

Lenten Peace

SUN PREFERENCE	CONTAINER SIZE	DIFFICULTY LEVEL
Shade	Medium	Easy

Shopping List

- Container mix potting soil
- 1 2-gallon-sized Christmas rose (*Helleborus argutifolius* 'Silver Lace') **A**
- 2 1-gallon-sized coral bells (*Heuchera* 'Silver Scrolls') **B**
- 3 1-gallon-sized camellias (*Camellia japonica* 'April Remembered') **C**
- 2 variegated Japanese sedges (*Carex morrowii* 'Aurea-variegata') **D**

There seems to be a calming effect that silver and white plants often provide, and the container recipe Lenten Peace combines an array of soothing season-long cool tones. Depending on your hardiness zone, *Helleborus* can begin blooming as early as late December, which you probably already figured out since one of its common names is Christmas rose. But this plant is also known as Lenten rose, most likely by colder zone cousins enjoying these blossoms during Lent in the spring. Sometime during the abundant display of the hellebore's upside-down blossoms, 'April Remembered' camellias begin their profusion of white flowers. Just as all this floriferous activity is starting to wind down, *Heuchera* 'Silver Scrolls' raises its wiry stems of pink-tinged white flowers to keep the display going. Even before all the blooms begin, the green, silver, and white foliage in this recipe provide an interesting display of textural beauty.

This recipe can be easily adapted to a window box as long as you don't have casement windows above the planter. Begin by filling the container about half way with container mix potting soil. Then make sure the plants that are farthest away from where you are standing or kneeling are placed first in the container. For the container pictured here, I stood in front of the container and planted the camellias first, followed by the *Carex*. Next, when planting the Lenten rose, slightly tilt the plants toward the front of the container. Place the coral bells and add more soil if need to cover the rootballs.

Watering is needed when the top of the soil is dry to touch. If you live in zones warmer than zone 6, this recipe also makes a nice winter or year-round planting. If you do keep this in the container for longer than two seasons, fertilize with a general-purpose fertilizer in late spring.

PLANT OPTIONS

If camellias are hard to come by, try 'Moonglow' juniper. You won't have the camellia flowers but the juniper's blue-gray tones will complement the other container ingredients.

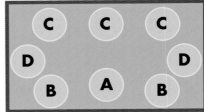

Red Twig Spring

SUN PREFERENCE	CONTAINER SIZE	DIFFICULTY LEVEL
Full Sun	Extra Large	Easy

Shopping List

- Container mix potting soil
- 3 3-gallon-sized red twig dogwoods (*Cornus stolonifera* 'Artic Fire') **A**
- 3 1-gallon-sized winter jasmines (*Jasminum nudiflorum*) **B**
- 3 1-quart-sized false cypress (*Chamaecyparis* 'Gold Pincushion') **C**
- 3 candytufts (*Iberis sempervirens* 'Alexander White') **D**
- 3 stonecrops (*Sedum* 'Angelina') **E**

It was past March 20, the "official" first day of spring, and I looked out my window to see snow on the ground. Feeling somewhat despondent for springtime, I stepped out to the back porch and there in my snow-dusted container was a planting that was defying the elements! This combination called Red Twig Spring is the *perfect* planting for those who want something blooming when very little else has started to bloom. Bright yellow trumpetlike flowers flow down the draping arms of the winter jasmine. *Iberis*, stirred to bloom by an earlier spell of warmer days, takes on the snow as if it were camouflage. The bronzy red hue that the 'Angelina' sedum takes on with colder weather only adds to the beauty.

Red twig dogwood is one plant that I rarely think about except when I'm planning something that needs winter interest. But it's a winner!

By late winter it will fully develop its winter glow and stands vibrantly against the new blooms of early spring. For zones 8 through 11, you may want to use *Acer palmatum* 'Sangokaku', which is most often referred to as a coral bark maple. This warmer climate area may also use white *Alyssum* instead of the *Iberis*. *Forsythia* 'Mindor' may perform better than the *Jasminum nudiflorum* in zones colder than zone 6. This cultivar is more compact and works well in a container.

All of the plants in this recipe are perennials or shrubs that you can allow to grow for several years in their container or install in your garden when you change the planter out for summer color. Remember to fertilize with a general-purpose fertilizer several times throughout the year if you use this as a year-round planting. Water only when soil is dry to the touch.

PLANT OPTIONS

If you have a hard time locating the Chamaecyparis *cultivar mentioned in the recipe, look for any low-growing juniper with golden color such as* Juniperus *'Daub's Frosted' or 'Gold Coast'.*

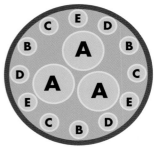

A Succulent Spring

Shopping List

- Container mix potting soil
- 1 small bag crushed volcanic rock or lava rock
- 1 echeveria (*Echeveria* 'Black Prince') **A**
- 1 stonecrop (*Sedeveria* hybrid 'Hummelii') **B**
- 1 stonecrop (*Sedum* hybrid 'Fine Gold Leaf') **C**

Every once in a while it is nice to have a little container planting that can either be placed on an outdoor tabletop or put on a small bare spot to add some interest. I saw this little planting combination at Saul Nursery in Atlanta, Georgia, and my love for succulent plants took off. This was planted within a carved stone container, but this same look can be achieved with any small shallow planter. There are an abundance of succulent plants to choose from to make a similar planter—just make sure you choose a succulent that will stay compact. Even though this recipe calls for using 4-inch plants, some *Sedum* species can get quite large over a short period of time.

Using just the soil that is around the rootball of the succulent, place these in the small container. If the depth of your container is deeper than the rootball, add a layer of crushed volcanic or lava rock along the bottom of your planter before positioning the plants. Fill in the spaces around the plants with crushed stone. *Sedum* species need very good drainage so this loose rock also helps ensure that water passes quickly through the container. If you choose a container that is deeper than the small stone planter shown here, add container mix potting soil to the planter with only the top three inches of the planter being filled with volcanic rock. Plant the succulent plants in this layer of rock. (Yes, really.)

These drought-tolerant plants do not need much fertilizing. About all that will be required for maintenance is a yearly sprinkle of granular all-purpose fertilizer each spring, and the random drink of water.

PLANT OPTIONS

A few succulent options to substitute that are happy in a wide range of zones are Sedum album *'Coral Carpet',* Sedum kamtschaticum *'Variegata', and* Sedum sexangulare *'Watch Chain'.*

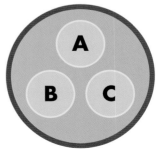

Sweetly Spring

SUN PREFERENCE	CONTAINER SIZE	DIFFICULTY LEVEL
Full Sun	Large	Moderate

Shopping List

- Container mix potting soil
- 5 diascia (*Diascia* hybrid Flying Colors® 'Trailing Antique Rose') **A**
- 3 snapdragons (*Antirrhinum* 'Sonnet Rose') **B**
- 5 pansies (*Viola* x *wittrockiana* 'Antique Shade') **C**
- 4 sweet William (*Dianthus barbatus* 'Cherry') **D**

Welcome spring with an array of pastel colors in a window box. I saw this combination while visiting Charleston, South Carolina, in late February—early spring for that part of the country. All of the plants in this window box can handle a light freeze with little signs of stress, which makes them a wonderful choice for a long season of spring color.

Not all diascia types trail as wonderfully as Flying Colors® 'Trailing Antique Rose', but *Diascia* plants do have a slightly trailing as well as mounding habit. One way to encourage plants to trail out of window boxes and containers is to plant them at a slight angle toward the outer edge of a container.

The biannual *Dianthus* is commonly called sweet William and has a slight clove-scented fragrance—*perfect* when keeping those windows open on delightful spring days. *Dianthus* and snapdragons rebloom best when their dead flower heads are removed on a regular basis (called "deadheading"). *Diascia* plants only need to be pinched back if they start to get a little leggy. All these prolific flowering plants will benefit from a monthly feeding of bloom-boosting fertilizer. Water only when the top of the soil is dry to touch. Keep a close eye on this planting if you experience a lot of spring rains and cool nights to see if you see any signs of pests or disease, which seem to like those cool, moist conditions. Check with your local Extension Service if you notice discolored leaves or other problems to see what treatment they would recommend for your area.

If you want more instant gratification when planting this window box, use 6-inch plants instead of the 4-inch plants in the recipe. This spring recipe could easily be a summer recipe for those in zones 2 through 4.

PLANT OPTIONS

For those in climates warmer than zone 7, a similar look can be achieved using rose-colored calibrachoa to replace the pansies and pink bacopa instead of the Diascia. Alyssum *and* Armeria *are two other spring-blooming varieties that offer pink blossoms, with the added benefit of the sweet alyssum's fragrance.*

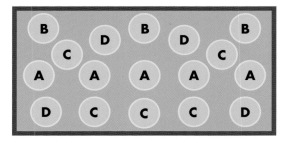

S
U
M
M
E
R

Above the Rest

SUN PREFERENCE
Full Sun

CONTAINER SIZE
Large

DIFFICULTY LEVEL
Intermediate

Shopping List

- Container mix potting soil
- Leather gardening gloves
- 1 Basket on a Stem (available from Kinsman Company)
- 1 1-gallon-sized agave (*Agave desmettiana* 'Variegated Dwarf') **A**
- 3 stonecrops (*Sedum reflexum* 'Angelina') **B**
- 3 stonecrops (*Sedum spurium* 'Dragon's Blood') **C**
- 3 1-gallon-sized purple pineapple lilies (*Eucomis comosa* 'Sparkling Burgundy') **D**
- 3 1-gallon-sized plumbagos (*Plumbago auriculata* 'Cape Blue') **E**
- 5 petunias (*Petunia* hybrid 'Baby Duck') **F**
- 5 petunias (*Petunia* hybrid 'Royal Magenta') **G**

Creating height in a large container can sometimes be cumbersome with large plant material. One option is to purchase a "Basket on a Stem" that will create a second level. Before adding potting mix to the container that will be the lower level, place the assembled Basket on a Stem in the middle of the planter. The Basket on a Stem has an 8-inch base at the bottom of the stem, which will help stabilize it after the potting mix is added. Fill the planter with container mix soil to within 6 inches of the top of the planter; then firmly press down all around it to support the stem.

Place the pineapple lilies around the stick, then add the plumbagos according to the diagram. Add more soil around the recently placed one-gallon *Eucomis* plants to secure them in their locations before adding the smaller plants. The soil will then be about 2½ inches from the top of the large planter and about 2 inches from the top of the rootballs of the pineapple lilies. Add the remaining plants according to the plant diagram. Fill in any gaps between plants with more soil mix.

A Basket on a Stem has a coco-liner that will need soil added to within 3 inches from the top. Plant the agave first in the middle of the basket. This is why the leather gloves are needed—agaves have some sharp leaves! *Carefully* plant the *Sedum* around the agave. The plants used in the small basket with the coco-liner will dry more quickly, but these plants are very drought tolerant (in fact, they thrive on less water) and need watering only half as often as the larger planter.

Water the larger planter only when the top of the soil feels dry to touch. Fertilize monthly with a bloom-boosting liquid fertilizer.

PLANT OPTIONS

If you can't find the Eucomis comosa, *try looking for* Cordyline 'Cabernett'. *An alternate for the petunias would be a calibrachoa (sometimes called million bells).*

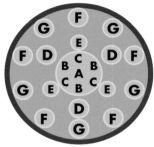

Attention Getter

SUN PREFERENCE	CONTAINER SIZE	DIFFICULTY LEVEL
Full Sun	Medium	Easy

Shopping List

- Container mix potting soil
- 1 1-gallon-sized dracaena palm (*Cordyline australis* 'Torbay Dazzler') **A**
- 4 geraniums (*Pelargonium* 'Caliente Fire') **B**
- 4 lantanas (*Lantana camara* 'Luscious® Citrus Blend™') **C**

Only plant this recipe if you want to bring attention to wherever this planter is located! The nonstop blooming of the 'Caliente Fire' geraniums and the lantanas, along with the exuberant display of the dracaena palm, will bring delight all summer long.

This recipe works well with a tall, thinner planter because of its wide growth habit, which makes the plants look as if they are exploding out of the planter. Begin by planting the *Cordyline* first, then the lantanas, and finally add the geraniums according to the planting diagram. Geraniums do *not* like to be planted too deeply so make sure that the potting mix is not mounding around the main stem of the plant that comes from the rootball. This variety of lantana is more mounding than trailing, and this variety of geranium is a hybrid between a mounding zonal geranium and a trailing ivy geranium. The result is that, even in a medium-sized planter, there is an extremely full effect that surrounds the more erect dracaena palm.

Pinch off any faded flowers from the geranium for a neater look, although this variety will keep blooming prolifically whether you pinch it back or not. Every plant in this recipe can take all day sun and doesn't mind being a little on the dry side. However, if you want to use this recipe in a part sun location, you may find that the lantana will go to seed more quickly. You will recognize this by the round, green seed balls that develop after the flower petals have fallen off. Simply keep these pinched off so that the plant spends its energy producing flowers and not seeds. Faithfully fertilizing this heavy blooming plant will keep it going strong throughout the summer.

The biggest danger to this recipe's success is overwatering after it is established. Some signs of overwatering are that the lantana will tend to go to seed and the leaves of the dracaena palm will start to rot at the base, making them very easy to pull out. When you do water, soak the soil to encourage the roots to grow deep into the pot, then allow the soil to dry until the top of the potting mix is dry to the touch.

PLANT OPTIONS

Create a softer look in this planter by using the green-and-white grass called Phalaris arundinacea *'Strawberries and Cream' instead of the* Cordyline. *Try* Bidens *'Peter's Gold Carpet' as a substitution for the lantana.*

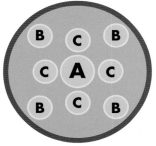

Beat The Heat

Shopping List

- Container mix potting soil
- 1 2-gallon-sized sago palm (*Cycas revoluta*) **A**
- 5 Swedish ivies (*Plectranthus coleoides* 'Variegata') **B**
- 5 ivy geraniums (*Pelargonium peltatum* 'Caliente Rose') **C**

Let me share a story of how well this recipe handles summertime heat. I planted the container shown here along with several others at a pool where I maintain the container plantings throughout the season. I traveled out of town for a week, but I gave specific instructions to my staff when to water all these different planters. Upon my return, I was anxious to see how all the new plantings had held up during the hot, dry week while I was away. I ran into one of my crew as he was just leaving from having watered in this area, and I asked him to walk around with me in case I had questions on their progress. When I came to this planting, I stuck my finger in the soil to test the moisture and was surprised to find that it was bone dry. My crewman sheepishly told me that this planter, which was in an out-of-the-way location, had been forgotten all week. I took the picture shown here on that day, a document to how resilient these three plants are to a little neglect.

Easy to put together, start by planting the sago palm, being careful to keep the rootball intact and the trunk above the soil line. The sago palm has a large, ball-like trunk that helps hold the fronds above the planter, allowing you a little more visibility of the underplantings. Surround the sago with the ivy geraniums, then circle these with the *Plectranthus* as indicated in the recipe diagram. The 'Caliente' series of geraniums hold true to their Spanish name, which means "hot" because they handle the heat beautifully.

Obviously from my description, you have probably gathered that this is a recipe that likes to be a little dry. Water your planter only when you can stick your finger up to the second joint into the soil and feel no moisture. Fertilize once a month with a bloom-boosting fertilizer for the ivy geraniums, which are heavy feeders. And if you go on vacation, make sure the folks watering for you know where all the containers are.

PLANT OPTIONS

For extreme drought resistance, substitute an Agave *'Blue Glow' for the sago palm. Keep the blue theme going by using* Plectranthus *'Nicolleta' rather than the 'Variegata' cultivar.*

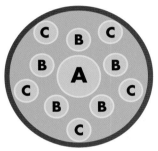

Best in Show

SUN PREFERENCE	CONTAINER SIZE	DIFFICULTY LEVEL
Partial Sun	Large	Easy

Shopping List

- Container mix potting soil
- 1 2-gallon-sized canna (*Canna generalis* 'Firecracker Red') **A**
- 3 hibiscus (*Hibiscus acetosella* 'Maple Sugar') **B**
- 4 red angelwing begonias (*Begonia* hybrid) **C**
- 9 periwinkles (*Vinca minor* 'Illumination') **D**
- 5 calibrachoas (*Calibrachoa* 'Trailing Blue') **E**

With an array of textures and colors to tickle your interest, get this recipe planted when the temperatures remain above 45 degrees F at night to watch the plants quickly intertwine and flourish. All the plants in Best in Show do well in a part sun location, even though the hibiscus and canna can also handle full sun when combined in other recipes.

Cannas have a thick, bulbous root system that expands quickly, which is why you want to make sure there is plenty of room in your large container for this plant to grow. Fill the planter with enough container mix soil so when you place the canna in the middle of the planter, the top of its rootball will be within one inch of the planter's top. Then, loosely fill in soil around the canna rootball and continue planting. The hibiscus grow very quickly so don't be surprised if you place your 4-inch plants next to the big leaves of the canna and they look kind of puny—that won't last very long; this recipe picture shows they will catch up.

When starting a planting in a large container like this with a heavily rooted plant in the middle, and the remaining plants are mostly 4-inch sized, you should train these smaller plants to send their roots toward the bottom of the container. How do you do that? Well, for the first two weeks, water once a day and saturate the soil. (Daytime and nighttime temperature affect the evaporation of the water so press the potting mix *firmly* with your fingers before watering each day. If water seeps around your fingers when pressing the soil, wait another day before watering. Potting soil that remains too wet will cause roots to rot.) After the first two weeks, water *only* when the top of the mix is dry to the touch.

Fertilize once a month with liquid bloom-boosting fertilizer. Pinch off any dead flowers from the canna for a neater look. This 'Maple Sugar' hibiscus blooms insignificantly and is utilized for its foliage.

PLANT OPTIONS

In a large container like this, you can substitute Black Lace™ elderberry, Sambucus nigra *'Eva', for the hibiscus or use* Arundo donax *'Peppermint Stick' instead of the canna for a more exotic look in your planter.*

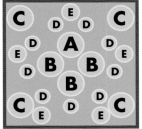

Big Hair Day

SUN PREFERENCE	CONTAINER SIZE	DIFFICULTY LEVEL
Full Sun	Medium	Easy

Shopping List

- Container mix potting soil
- 1 2-gallon-sized sago palm (*Cycas revoluta*) **A**
- 3 alyssum (*Lobularia* hybrid 'Snow Princess') **B**
- 6 geraniums (*Pelargonium* 'Caliente Fire') **C**

When it comes to easy care, this will rank close to the succulent bowl container planting (page 44). I planted this recipe at a location where the client *completely* forgot about it for more than a month. Fortunately, we had a few rains to ensure that it lived, but that was the only water the plants received. When I returned and asked about the planters, he quickly realized he had forgotten about them; we both ran to see how dried out they were. Though the *Lobularia* and geraniums had lost all their blooms, they quickly rejuvenated over the next few weeks of faithful watering. Now, don't go trying this at your house! (Note: if plants have been stressed due to underwatering or extreme heat, resist the urge to fertilize. Only begin fertilizing again after a week of healthy care.)

Start this recipe by planting the sago palm in the container partially filled with soil. This is one of the few times that I recommend planting the rootball so that the root top is parallel to the rim of the container. Add more potting mix around the rootball, leaving enough space for the remaining plants to be added according the recipe diagram. These smaller plants still need to be an inch below the container rim.

As far as watering is concerned, keep this planting on the dry side. The *Lobularia* will be the indicator plants that water is needed as they will become noticeably droopy when underwatered. Fertilize monthly with a bloom-boosting fertilizer and pinch off the stems from dead geraniums.

Sago palms can be brought indoors during the winter months and grown as a houseplant if they are kept in a sunny location. I recommend removing the annual flowers and replanting in a smaller well-draining container with just enough soil to cover the rootball. Water lightly once a week.

PLANT OPTIONS

Calm the Big Hair Day down with Euphorbia *'Diamond Frost' or*
Scaevola *'Bombay White' instead of the alyssum.*

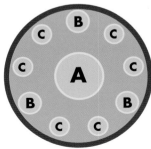

The Black Pearl

SUN PREFERENCE
Partial Sun

CONTAINER SIZE
Medium

DIFFICULTY LEVEL
Easy

Shopping List

- Container mix potting soil
- 1 1-gallon-sized ornamental pepper (*Capsicum annuum* 'Black Pearl') **A**
- 5 dwarf dahlias (*Dahlia* 'Harlequin Mix') **B**
- 5 calibrachoas (*Calibrachoa* 'Trailing Blue') **C**

This recipe title may bring to mind visions of marauding pirates and swashbuckling adventures, but this little planting full of color and contrast is really a pleasant companion to have in your garden. I enjoy watching how this recipe changes throughout the season, as the ornamental peppers turn from black to red and the dahlias open with a mix of red, purple, orange, and yellow flowers. But don't be fooled by the sweet looking peppers—they hold a surprise attack of fiery taste!

Center the pepper in the middle of the medium-sized container, then surround it with the dahlias as shown in the recipe diagram. Plant the dahlias at a slight angle toward the outside edge of the container. Finally, place the calibrachoas following the recipe layout. Depending on the fullness of the plants that you purchased, this container may look a little sparse when it's first planted. The dahlias and calibrachoas fill in quickly, and the dahlias actually bloom best when they have a little space to spread out.

None of these plants like to stay in overly moist soil. Let the top one inch of soil dry out before watering again. The best way to test for this is to stick your finger in the soil up to first joint to check for moisture. You can also tell when the plants need watering if the calibrachoas' leaves appear curled or limp; they will be the first plants that tend to dry out of these three varieties. Fertilize once a month with a bloom-boosting fertilizer. This recipe is listed for part sun but those growing in zones 6 and colder will find these plants do just fine in full sun locations also.

And if The Black Pearl still has you hankering to join the pirate's life, put on an eye patch, pull out your pruning shears, and with a flourish cry, "Off with their heads!" as you prune off the faded dahlia blooms. Just don't let the neighbors see you.

PLANT OPTIONS

If growing dahlias makes you a little anxious (they sometimes get a bad rap for being difficult to maintain), use Zinnia 'Short Stuff' mix or 'Profusion' mix. Calibrachoas can be substituted by blue verbenas or blue fan flowers.

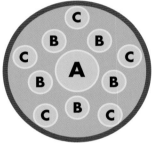

Bloomin' Crazy

SUN PREFERENCE	CONTAINER SIZE	DIFFICULTY LEVEL
Full Sun	Large	Easy

Shopping List

- Container mix potting soil
- 1 3-gallon-sized tropical hibiscus (*Hibiscus rosa-sinensis* 'Full Moon®') **A**
- 3 phlox (*Phlox* hybrid 'Intensia® Cabernet') **B**
- 6 calibrachoas (*Calibrachoa* 'Trailing Blue') **C**
- 3 lantanas (*Lantana* 'Anne Marie') **D**
- 3 chameleon plants (*Houttuynia cordata* 'Chameleon') **E**

One of the benefits of this container recipe is that something is going on all over the container, at all times. With the appeal of a three-ring circus, there are frilly yellow flowers suspended above all the action below, phlox blossoms are popping their heads through the array of color, and the unpredictable chameleon plants keep us entertained with its cheery ever-changing foliage. Just get this planted and sit back to watch the show.

Depending on the size of your planter, you'll only want to fill it about two-thirds full of container mix potting soil before you start planting. Take the hibiscus and shave off about one inch around the rootball, then place in the container as shown in the recipe diagram. Add more mix around the roots of the hibiscus, followed by planting the phlox and lantanas. Next, position the chameleon plants and the calibrachoas for that final touch of color. Check to see if you need additional soil to fill in any spaces between the plants' roots.

This container recipe does best with evenly moist soil, meaning that the soil does not dry out to the point where it starts to pull away from the sides of the container. If the top of the soil feels dry to the touch, it is time to water again. Yellow leaves on the hibiscus are usually indicators that the recipe is getting too much water so if this occurs, you will want to back off a little on the watering and add a fertilizer that contains some iron. Once or twice throughout the summer, trim an inch or two off the end of the calibrachoas to encourage blooming along the branches. Also, pick up any fallen hibiscus blooms that land on the plants below so that they aren't smothered under the old blooms. Fertilize once a month with a bloom-boosting plant food.

PLANT OPTIONS

Yellow bush allamanda could be used instead of the hibiscus; Angelonia 'Dark Plum' is a good substitute for the phlox; and sweet potato vine Ipomoea 'Tri-color' could be exchanged for the chameleon plants.

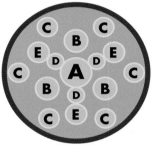

Blushing Basket

SUN PREFERENCE	CONTAINER SIZE	DIFFICULTY LEVEL
Full Sun	Medium	Easy

Shopping List

- Container mix potting soil
- 1 clean, disposable 8-inch aluminum pie plate
- 1 20-inch hanging basket with coco or moss liner
- 1 1-gallon-sized diplandenia (*Mandevilla splendens* 'Red Riding Hood') **A**
- 5 ivy geraniums (*Pelargonium peltatum* 'Blizzard Blue') **B**
- 5 ivy geraniums (*Pelargonium peltatum* 'Freestyle Ruby Red') **C**

Hanging baskets can often be difficult to maintain because of their exposure to wind *and* sun, but this recipe will take away some of that frustration. One of the keys to success is choosing the right drought tolerant plants. The other is providing a way to keep water from seeping out too quickly.

Before adding any container mix potting soil into the hanging basket, take the pie plate and place on the bottom of the hanging basket. If you have an empty planter that is 16 to 20 inches wide, plop your basket in another container while you are planting. Loosely fill the basket with soil and plant the diplandenia. Add geraniums according to the plant diagram. Both 'Blizzard' and 'Freestyle' varieties of ivy geranium seem to thrive in the heat so if you plant these 4-inch plants while the temperatures are still in the 50s and 60s, you may not see them grow much until the daytime temperatures get warmer.

Do not let these plants sit in consistently moist soil. Let soil slightly dry out (but not so dry that the soil pulls away from the sides of the basket) before watering again. All plants in this recipe are self-cleaning, which means that they don't need to be deadheaded before they will flower again. But the geraniums will have a neater look if you pinch off the stems of dead flowers. Geraniums also respond better to being pinched by hand than with pruners. The diplandenia, while generally a bushy type plant, will sometimes send a tendril or two to climb up along the chains of the hanging basket. These are all sun loving plants so place them where they can soak up the sunshine. The diplandenia is a true tropical, which means that it handles the extreme heat (upper 90s and 100s) without much stress. However, even ivy geraniums will need some afternoon shade in those types of temperatures.

These guys are heavy feeders, so keep them well fed with a bloom-boosting monthly fertilizer.

PLANT OPTIONS

If you start substituting plants in this recipe, you'll have a whole new recipe. That being said, you can still exchange the diplandenia by Angelonia *'Angelmist™ Dark Pink' to lighten the texture of this combination.*

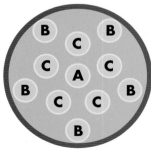

Bougainvillea Boogie

SUN PREFERENCE	CONTAINER SIZE	DIFFICULTY LEVEL
Full Sun	Extra Large	Intermediate

Shopping List

- Container mix potting soil
- 1 5-gallon-sized trellised bougainvillea (*Bougainvillea* 'Barbara Karst') **A**
- 3 2-gallon-sized cannas (*Canna* 'Minerva') **B**
- 3 2-gallon-sized bougainvilleas (*Bougainvillea* 'Raspberry Ice') **C**
- 6 sweet potato vines (*Ipomoea batatas* 'Blackie') **D**
- 6 1-gallon-sized elephant ears (*Colocasia* 'Illustris') **E**

When one of my co-workers first described this recipe to me, I wasn't too sure how all this would come together. But I found the dark foliage juxtaposed against the display of blooming reds, yellows, and purples of this recipe quite appealing. Another practical reason this recipe works is the fact that the thick rooted cannas will have lots of room to spread out in this extra-large planter.

Fill your planter only about halfway with container mix potting soil before you begin planting. Start assembling this recipe by placing the five-gallon-sized trellised bougainvillea in the middle of the planter. You may want to wear gloves and long sleeves when planting because bougainvillea has a few thorns. Next, plant the cannas and the 'Raspberry Ice' bougainvilleas to keep the trellised bougainvillea from falling over in the container. At this point you may need

to add more potting mix before planting the remaining ingredients. Place the *Colocasia* and sweet potato vines in the container as indicated by the recipe diagram, finishing with additional soil that may be needed to cover all of the plants' roots.

After all has been planted, you may look at your handiwork and wonder, "What have I done wrong?" The planting may look a little sparse today but will most likely be overflowing in a few weeks. Any empty space will soon be filled be sweet potato vine foliage and the cannas filling out their space. In fact, your maintenance will include periodically trimming back the sweet potato vines (if you wish) and cutting off the old flowers from the abundant flow of blooms on the cannas. Fertilize with a general-purpose plant food once a month and water when the top two inches of soil are dry to the touch.

PLANT OPTIONS

Lemongrass, Cymbopogon, *would make an interesting alternative to the cannas in this recipe, and a trellised red passionflower,* Passiflora manicata, *could be used instead of the trellised bougainvillea.*

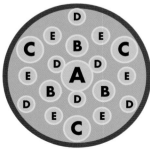

Bravo

SUN PREFERENCE	CONTAINER SIZE	DIFFICULTY LEVEL
Full Sun	Medium	Easy

Shopping List

- Container mix potting soil
- 1 3-gallon-sized bush allamanda (*Allamanda nerifolia* 'Yellow') **A**
- 6 trailing petunias (*Petunia* hybrid 'Suncatcher Burgundy') **B**
- 6 calibrachoas (*Calibrachoa* hybrid 'Cabernet Purple') **C**

The words *rich* and *vibrant color* come to mind when looking at this container recipe. Bush allamanda is often overlooked during spring plantings because it doesn't have much character until it starts to get hot. But once this plant gets a taste of 70 degree F weather, those yellow trumpet flowers start popping out all over.

When filling the planter with container mix potting soil, leave room to place the 3-gallon rootball of the allamanda. After loosening the soil around its roots, place the allamanda in the planter and continue adding soil mix until the soil is about 1 ½ inches below the rim of the container. Continue planting the petunias and calibrachoas according to the diagram.

One of the beautiful qualities found in many of the newer varieties of petunia is their multi-branching property, which mean low maintenance petunias—no more summer-long pinching back on those leggy branches and getting a sticky mess all over your hands. 'Suncatcher Burgundy' is a variety that mounds and trails nicely without taking over the planter. Calibrachoa, with all its wide, wonderful arrays of color and prolific blooming, can be unforgiving if the soil is allowed to dry out completely, so keep an eye on this plant and water at the first sign of wilting. On the other hand, none of these plants like to be in moist soil so care must be taken not to overwater.

With this much constant flowering going on, fertilizing with one-quarter strength liquid bloom-boosting fertilizer as often as once a week is beneficial. In extreme temperatures, both the calibrachoas and petunias will need protection from afternoon sun.

PLANT OPTIONS

Try Rudbeckia *'Tiger Eye' or* Helenium amarum *'Dakota Gold' as
an option for bush allamanda for cooler climates.* Bougainvillea *and*
Evolvulus *can substitute for the petunias or calibrachoas in hotter climes.*

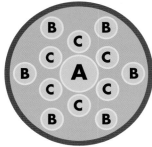

Bright Spot

SUN PREFERENCE	CONTAINER SIZE	DIFFICULTY LEVEL
Full Sun	Large	Easy

Shopping List

- Container mix potting soil
- 3 1-gallon-sized black-eyed Susans (*Rudbeckia hirta* 'Indian Summer') **A**
- 3 cupheas (*Cuphea llavea* 'Flamenco Samba') **B**
- 3 trailing verbenas (*Verbena* hybrid 'Tukana Scarlet') **C**
- 3 petunias (*Petunia* hybrid 'Royal Velvet') **D**

Let me start this description by confessing my love for *Cuphea* 'Flamenco Samba'. This cuphea is often overlooked in the nursery centers because until it blooms it looks a little like a lanky weed. But hold on to your hat, because when this baby starts blooming it will blow you away! The key to getting the most out of this variety of cuphea is to put it in the hottest, sunniest spot you have. I've seen this cuphea handle 100 degree F days, perk back up after being underwatered, and *still* look good after being hit with a light frost.

After loosely filling your container with soil, leaving about three inches from the rim of the planter to the top of the soil, plant the 1-gallon-sized *Rudbeckia* followed by the remaining plants according to the recipe diagram. All the rootball tops should be about one inch from the rim of the planter at this point. This is a recipe that if planted in the early cooler days of summer or spring, may look a little puny for the first week or two. But patience wins out—when the temperatures start rising, the blossoms will follow.

Fertilize monthly with bloom-boosting plant food and snip off the stems of old *Rudbeckia* flowers. This *Rudbeckia* also makes a nice, long-lasting cut flower for floral arrangements or to simply enjoy in a vase in your home. Verbenas will sometimes rest from blooming if the temperatures remain for several weeks in the upper 90 to 100 degree F range, but fortunately the cupheas will keep providing the red needed in this recipe. Water when the top of the soil is dry to your touch. The black-eyed Susans are good indicator plants to let you know when this container needs watering because the leaves will be noticeably droopy. If you notice them drooping, be sure to give the planting a good soaking to saturate the soil.

Gardeners in cooler, wetter climates may not experience the love affair I've had with cuphea, but I encourage you to try it at least once!

PLANT OPTIONS

Want to mix things up a little more while still using the same color scheme? Try using Hemerocallis *'Happy Returns' daylily instead of the* Rudbeckia *for more foliage contrast. Just keep in mind that the blossoms are more yellow than the gold color of the* Rudbeckia.

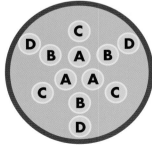

Call Me Summertime

Shopping List

- Container mix potting soil
- 1 kitchen-sized trash bag
- 2 1-gallon-sized variegated gingers (*Alpinia zerumbet* 'Variegata') **A**
- 2 1-gallon-sized mandevillas (*Mandevilla* hybrid 'Sun Parasol Crimson') **B**
- 4 zinnias (*Zinnia marylandica* 'Zahara Yellow') **C**
- 6 petunias (*Petunia* hybrid 'Royal Velvet') **D**
- 2 trailing verbenas (*Verbena* hybrid 'Tukana Scarlet') **E**
- 2 lantanas (*Lantana camara* 'New Gold') **F**
- 2 petunias (*Petunia* hybrid 'Surfinia Lavender Lace') **G**

Don't ever plan on being bored with Call Me Summertime. Just when you think you know what it is going to look like, a heat wave will come along and as the red verbenas rest from blooming the gold lantanas will come on strong.

Layer the inside bottom of a coco-liner hayrack planter with a trash bag that has 6 or 7 ¼-inch holes poked through the bag. Do not poke holes through the coco-liner. Add the trash bag liner only on window boxes with coco-liners or moss liners. When adding soil, remember to leave room for four 1-gallon-sized plants.

One of the tips to planting window boxes is to start with the area farthest away from where you are standing. For the recipe pictured here I stood in front of the window box and started by planting the ginger, then adding the mandevilla on either side of the ginger. If I were planting from inside, I would have planted the 'Royal Velvet' petunias and zinnias first, then planted the trailing plants out the front before planting the mandevillas and finally the variegated gingers.

This large planter can get very heavy when fully planted and watered so verify that whomever installs the planters knows how to secure them safely to your window or balcony railing.

Many of the plants in this recipe are sun loving but they can perform well in the part sun requirements needed for the variegated ginger. Petunias can feel the stress of heat in warmer climates so the part sun requirement will keep them looking better in those environments. Water when soil is dry to the touch or when you see the variegated ginger leaves start to curl. Fertilize once a month with a bloom-boosting plant food.

PLANT OPTIONS

Since variegated ginger can be hard to locate in some areas, consider using Euonymus *'Emerald Gaiety' or a green-and-yellow coleus such as 'Wild Lime' or 'Collins Gold'.*

Canna Fans

Shopping List

- Container mix potting soil
- 1 1-gallon-sized canna (*Canna* 'Australia') **A**
- 5 coleus (*Solenostemon scutellarioides* 'Wizard Scarlet') **B**
- 5 fan flowers (*Scaevola aemula* 'New Wonder') **C**

Dark foliage can be a powerful asset in turning a simple planting into a dramatic showpiece. These three plant choices provide summer-long enjoyment with very low maintenance. The color echoes in this recipe are both subtle and distinct. There is the strong echo of burgundy in the coleus and canna leaves, then the subtle echo of yellow found in the edges of the coleus leaves and the eyes of the *Scaevola's* fan shaped flowers. As the summer progresses, the blue flowers of the coleus will echo the blue *Scaevola*. I recommend that you faithfully pinch back the flowers of the coleus until late summer to maintain a thick growth of foliage.

Cannas have a very dense, bulbous root system that expand quickly so even in a medium-sized planter you will want to only use a 1- or 2-gallon-sized plant. I have seen the root systems of cannas break apart pots because there was no room left for them to grow during the summer. Place the canna in the container that has been partially filled with potting soil, adding more as needed to stabilize the roots in the pots. Finish planting the coleus and fan flowers according to recipe diagram.

Water this planting when the top of the soil feels dry to your touch. *Scaevola* and canna both can tolerate full sun conditions but will perform just as well in this location when paired with a coleus that requires part sun conditions. Fertilize once a month with a bloom-boosting plant food. Snip off the dead flowers of the canna throughout the summer to keep it fresh looking and encourage reblooming. Cannas start blooming in early summer and will keep blooming all summer if they're fertilized regularly. Even where cannas are hardy, I would not recommend leaving it to overwinter in the summer container because of how quickly the roots can expand and risk damaging the container. To overwinter the canna, cut back all the leaves, remove it from the planter, and place it in a plastic pot that will hold the roots, and lightly cover in mulch or sawdust. Store in a cool, dry spot.

PLANT OPTIONS

When you only have three plants in a recipe, substitutions end up creating a whole new recipe. But if you are a fan of foliage only plants, substitute the sweet potato vine cultivar Ipomoea batatas *'Sweet Caroline Green Yellow' for the* Scaevola.

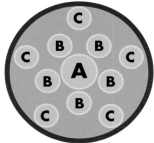

Don't Think Twice Bowl

SUN PREFERENCE	CONTAINER SIZE	DIFFICULTY LEVEL
Full Sun	Medium	Easy

Shopping List

- Container mix potting soil
- Crushed gravel, small pebbles, or clean sand
- 1 blue agave (*Agave weberi*) **A**
- 2 stonecrops (*Sedum rupestre* 'Lemon Ball') **B**
- 2 stonecrops (*Sedum rupestre* 'Variegated') **C**
- 2 hens and chicks (*Sempervivum*) **D**
- 4 jade plants (*Crassula* 'Campfire') **E**
- 2 Chinese sedums (*Sedum tetractinum*) **F**

There is more than one reason why this recipe is called Don't Think Twice Bowl. First, once these succulent plants become rooted in, you rarely have to think twice about watering them. Second, even though there are several varieties of succulents listed in this recipe, don't think twice if you want to substitute some other variety of low-growing succulent to fill your bowl. Check the plant tags to see if certain succulents have different sun requirements and choose plants that all have the same requirement. For example, if you want a succulent bowl to leave on a covered porch table, choose succulent plants that can grow in the shade.

Even though entire books have been written about succulent plantings, there are only a few points to remember when potting up succulents. In a *well-draining* planter, I like to use the same container mix potting soil to plant my succulents as I do other plants. While succulents are very drought tolerant and low maintenance, they still can benefit from the nutrients in a good potting mix. After planting all the succulents in the container, add a thin layer of sand, crushed gravel, or small pebbles on top of the mix. All newly installed plants need to be watered, succulents or not, so give this new planting a drink of water every other day for the first week. Succulents don't need a lot of fertilizer. But, by midsummer you may want to give this recipe a diluted application of a general-purpose fertilizer.

You can also consider making this a year-round succulent planting. Look for succulents that are hardy in your zone and use only those varieties for your planting. Or consider bringing the bowl indoors for the winter; with as little watering as is needed for these plants, they would like the warm, dry air of a heated home.

PLANT OPTIONS

*The options for substitution in this "no worries" container recipe are
endless, but here are a few evergreen sedums for a year-round sedum
bowl:* Sedum repestre *'Blue Spruce',* Sedum spurium *'Dragon's
Blood',* or Sedum *'Angelina'.*

Don't Underestimate Me

SUN PREFERENCE	CONTAINER SIZE	DIFFICULTY LEVEL
Shade	Large	Easy

Shopping List

- Container mix potting soil
- 1 3-gallon-sized Hawaiian ti (*Cordyline fruticosa* 'Black Magic') **A**
- 9 wishbone flowers (*Torenia* 'Golden Moon') **B**
- 8 impatiens (*Impatiens* hybrid 'Butterfly Deep Pink') **C**

Another name for this recipe could be The Three Shade Plants That Never Give Up. To be such delicate looking plants, these three varieties have proven to be summertime workhorses—as long as they stay out of the afternoon sun. The biggest stress factor I've seen with this recipe has been when these plants are placed in a very windy location; the *Cordyline* gets quite battered looking. I've found them all underwatered in different containers and watched with amazement at how they rebounded with several days of consistent watering.

Begin planting this recipe by making sure you leave room for the ti plant's rootball when pouring the container mix potting soil into the planter. Once it has been positioned in the middle of the planter, add soil mix loosely around the rootball and continue planting the impatiens and *Torenia* according to the recipe diagram. This large container may look a little sparse at first with the 4-inch plants, but both the impatiens and *Torenia* grow rapidly to fill in any empty spaces. The impatiens would also benefit

from a gentle pinching of one or two inches off the top of the plants to encourage them to bush out more. This can be done at planting and then about forty-five days later. 'Butterfly Deep Pink' has a smaller flower than many impatiens but redeems itself with a plethora of smaller flowers that cover the planting.

The more morning sun that this recipe receives, the more water it will need for the plants to remain healthy. While quite content with dappled shade or a couple of hours of early morning sun, this container recipe tolerates sun up until noon except in very hot climates. Keeping the soil evenly moist seems to be the key to success for impatiens, *Torenia*, and this variety of *Cordyline*.

Cordyline fruticosa 'Black Magic' is sometimes used as an indoor plant. After removing the summer annuals, replant it in a smaller planter that can be placed in a sunny area of your home. Keep the planter away from drafts and the drying effects of heater vents. Then, replant again the following summer for outside pleasure.

PLANT OPTIONS

Create a bolder look in this recipe simply by adding Begonia *'Dragonwing™ Red' instead of the impatiens. You can also create a more dramatic look by switching out the* Cordyline *by* Alocasia infernalis *'Kapit' or* Colocasia *'Black Magic'.*

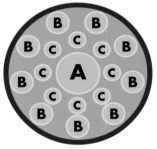

Doorway Delight

SUN PREFERENCE	CONTAINER SIZE	DIFFICULTY LEVEL
Shade	Medium	Moderate

Shopping List

- Container mix potting soil
- 1 1-gallon-sized dracaena palm (*Cordyline* 'Southern Splendor') **A**
- 1 wishbone flower (*Torenia* hybrid 'Summer Wave Blue') **B**
- 1 asparagus fern (*Asparagus sprengeri*) **C**
- 2 trailing coleus (*Solenostemon scutellarioides* 'Strawberry Drop') **D**
- 3 double impatiens (*Impatiens walleriana* 'Rockapulco Rose') **E**

With all the colorful foliage in this recipe, flowers seem to be an afterthought! This shade loving combination provides height and volume even with a medium-sized container. One reason I like to use plants in the *Cordyline* family is because their blades are stiff enough to allow other plants to weave in and up the plant, acting almost like a natural trellis for other trailing plants.

Fill the container loosely with soil, then first plant the *Cordyline* to ensure that it is positioned correctly according to the recipe diagram. Add the remaining plants as indicated by the diagram. Check to make sure that all the tops of the rootballs on the plants are about one inch below the rim of the planter. Add any potting mix to fill in space between plants.

This recipe is not quite as drought tolerant as many of the other summer recipes mentioned in this book. Look to the impatiens as the indicator plants that extra water is needed; they will droop noticeably when the soil is too dry. Keep this planting evenly moist, meaning that you don't want the soil to completely dry out but you also don't want it to remain soggy. Fertilize with a general-purpose fertilizer once a month.

Throughout the summer you will notice the coleus developing lovely stems of blue flowers. If allowed to flower the coleus will become leggier and stretched out. Keep pinching these flowers off until late summer to encourage the coleus to become fuller. Then as fall approaches allow the coleus to bloom on the multiple branches that have developed through the summer. The display of blue flowers is delightful and will echo the blue of the wishbone flower.

Have you ever wondered why *Torenia* is called wishbone flower? Take a look inside one of the flowers and see if you can find what that looks like a miniature version of a turkey wishbone.

PLANT OPTIONS

Maintain a more monochrome look by switching out the Cordyline *with* Pennisetum *'Princess Molly'. Alternatively, you can brighten up the look with* Solenostemon *'Trailing Green Olives' rather than using 'Strawberry Drop'.*

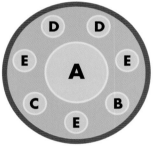

Everything's Rosy

SUN PREFERENCE	CONTAINER SIZE	DIFFICULTY LEVEL
Full Sun	Medium	Moderate

Shopping List

- Container mix potting soil
- 2 1-gallon-sized shrub roses (*Rosa* 'Home Run') **A**
- 3 euphorbias (*Euphorbia* 'Diamond Frost') **B**
- 4 heirloom geraniums (*Pelargonium hortorum* 'Wilhellm Langguth') **C**
- 3 coleus (*Solenostemon scutellarioides* 'Strawberry Drop') **D**

Don't think roses should be delegated only to the landscape. The low, bushy profiles of these 'Home Run' roses make them an excellent choice to use in container plantings. This rose variety proves to be a true red with excellent powdery mildew resistance *plus* it blooms all summer long.

When putting together this recipe, I recommend wearing a long-sleeved shirt plus your normal gardening gloves. The 'Home Run' rose is as thorny as it is beautiful and disease resistant. Fill your planter loosely with container mix potting soil, leaving about 3 or 4 inches between the soil and the rim of the container. Plant the roses according to the recipe diagram and add more soil if needed so that the remaining plants can be planted. The soil should now be about 1 inch below the rim of the planter and should barely be covering the tops of all the plants' rootballs.

When first planted, this recipe may look a little sparse. The 'Home Run' rose will need space to fill out, which it does rather quickly. The color echo of the white euphorbias and the variegated foliage of the geraniums is made even more interesting because of the contrast in texture of the euphorbia's flower and the large, round geranium leaves. Pops of red are repeated by the 'Home Run' roses, the geraniums, and the coleus.

All of the plants in this recipe like to be on the dry side after the first two weeks of planting. Those first two weeks of getting plants established in their planter usually requires a daily watering. After those first two weeks, allow the top 2 inches of soil to dry out before watering again. Use a specialized rose fertilizer to feed the plants in this container, following the instructions for frequency of use but use only at half strength. For example, fertilize at the same intervals of time but if the instructions say to use one cup of fertilizer, use only one-half cup.

PLANT OPTIONS

Go for a clean, crisp look by substituting a red rose for Flower Carpet® White groundcover rose and using Plectranthus 'Variegata' instead of the heirloom geranium.

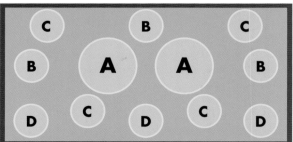

The Ferny Queen

Shopping List

- Container mix potting soil
- 1 3-gallon-sized fern (*Nephrolepis obliterata* 'Kimberly Queen') **A**
- 3 euphorbias (*Euphorbia* 'Diamond Frost') **B**
- 3 ivy geraniums (*Pelargonium* 'Taj Mahal') **C**
- 3 calibrachoas (*Calibrachoa* 'Trailing Blue') **D**
- 3 chocolate moneywort (*Lysimachia congestiflora* 'Persian Chocolate') **E**
- 3 calibrachoas (*Calibrachoa* 'Saffron') **F**

If you've never used ferns in container plantings before, either because you heard that they shed or don't like sun or because they simply are just green, then let me introduce you to the queen of ferns. *Nephrolepis obliterata*, which is much more easily and commonly called 'Kimberly Queen' fern or the less common name of Australian sword fern, regally holds its fronds upright, inviting a display of summer color to be planted beneath it. 'Kimberly Queen' fern can be used in full sun or part sun such as in this recipe, and it is one of the few tropical ferns that can tolerate dry conditions.

When filling the container with soil in this recipe, leave room for the large rootball of the 'Kimberly Queen' fern. Usually by the time this fern reaches 3-gallon size, its root system is very dense, which means that reducing the size of the

rootball can be a little more difficult. You can take the edge of a trowel or use a hori-hori gardening knife to loosen the roots of the fern before planting so that there will be more room for the remaining plants. With some of the 3-gallon-sized 'Kimberly Queen' ferns that I've planted, I divided the rootball in half using a shovel or garden fork and used the 2 halves in two separate containers. This fern grows quickly and is thick enough that dividing it will have very little effect on the finished look of this recipe.

Water only when the top of the soil is dry to the touch. The plants in this recipe do not like to be overwatered so let the calibrachoas be the indicator plants; if you see the leaves slightly wilting it is time to give the planting a long drink of water. Fertilize monthly with a bloom-boosting fertilizer.

PLANT OPTIONS

Nephrolepis biserrat *'Macho'* ferns can be substituted for the *'Kimberly Queen'* fern. Petunia *'Baby Duck'* and Petunia *'Royal Velvet'* are options if the calibrachoa varieties are not available.

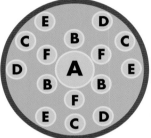

Fiery Banana Bowl

SUN PREFERENCE	CONTAINER SIZE	DIFFICULTY LEVEL
Partial Sun	Large	Easy

Shopping List

- Container mix potting soil
- 1 3-gallon-sized banana tree (*Musa basjoo*) **A**
- 5 lantanas (*Lantana* hybrid 'Patriot™ Desert Sunset') **B**
- 5 coleus (*Solenostemon* 'Trailing Rose') **C**

When I first saw this container combination in Kansas at Family Tree Nursery, it took my breath away. Majestic and tropical looking, my first thought was, "We're not in Kansas anymore, Toto." Okay, maybe that wasn't my first thought, but I definitely thought that this was a recipe worth repeating. To provide such a vivid display, it really is an amazingly simple plant combination.

Place the banana tree as indicated by the diagram into your container, and, depending on your container size, add potting mix as needed so that the top of the rootball on the banana is about one inch below the level of the container's rim. Add more mix around the rootball of the banana tree, bringing the level of the soil to within two to three inches of the top of the rootball. Now, add the lantana, then the coleus, tilting the coleus slightly toward the outer rim of the container. After planting all this in your large container,

you may be a little disappointed that your planting doesn't *quite* look like the photo shown here. Both the coleus and lantanas will take off, growing quickly once they're planted in your container and you'll be pinching off coleus blooms before you know it. Pinching off the blue flower spikes of the coleus will force more branching, making a denser display of that wonderful coleus foliage.

If you notice the lantanas going to seed, which happens when you see small, round green seedheads clustered around where the old blooms were located, pinch these off to encourage the plants to spend their energy making blooms and not seed. Use a general-purpose fertilizer once a month and water when the top two inches of soil are dry to the touch. Cut off any old or windswept banana leaves at the base of the leaf next to the stalk.

PLANT OPTIONS

Using Canna *'Wyoming'*
instead of the banana tree will
give you a similar look, and
will add an extra pop of color
with the orange canna flowers.
Orange crossandra could be
substituted for the lantana.

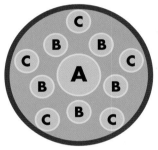

Foxy Medusa

SUN PREFERENCE	CONTAINER SIZE	DIFFICULTY LEVEL
Full Sun	Medium	Moderate

Shopping List

- Container mix potting soil
- 1 1-gallon-sized foxtail fern (*Asparagus densiflorus* 'Myers') **A**
- 5 purple queen (*Setcreasea pallida*) **B**
- 5 calibrachoas (*Calibrachoa* hybrid 'Superbells Blue') **c**

Here's a Medusa that you don't need to be afraid of, and you can look at it all you like without turning into stone. *Asparagus* 'Myers', or foxtail fern as it is most commonly called, has enough character to be used in a container all on its own. Drought tolerant and low maintenance, this recipe brings a bit of whimsy to a garden with its wild-hair look.

Foxtail fern has a massive and tuberous root system, which makes it drought resistant but also makes it somewhat of a hog in the container. Don't be hesitant if this one-gallon-sized plant starts out looking a little small in the medium-sized container—its foliage will quickly fill out and it will need the container space for its water-holding tubers. Plant this first in your partially soil-filled container, then add more soil loosely around the rootball before placing the remaining plants called for in this recipe. *Setcreasea*, another drought resistant plant, seems to echo the Medusa theme with its thick blades of untamed foliage. The calibrachoas are the only somewhat polite plants in this trio, draping nicely over the edges with their continually blooming blue flowers.

In this recipe the calibrachoas will be the indicator plants that water is needed. None of the plants in Foxy Medusa does very well in moist soil, but just be careful not to let the calibrachoas dry out. If the top of the soil is dry to your touch and the leaves of the calibrachoas start to droop or slightly curl, give the planting a good, long drink of water. Then allow the soil to dry again until the top feels dry to the touch. If you press gently into the soil about a half inch and feel any moisture, then it is too soon to water again.

The plants in this recipe do not need to be pitched or pruned back unless you want to control their prolific growth. Fertilize once a month with a bloom-boosting plant food to keep the calibrachoas in full flower. In the photo used here to display the recipe, this planter was placed in front of a red wax begonia that is often used in landscaping. I have often substituted the calibrachoas in this recipe with this same type begonia for a very low maintenance planting.

PLANT OPTIONS

If you want an alternate for the Asparagus *'Myers', try using* Nephrolepis obliterata *'Kimberly Queen' fern. Some really good options for the calibrachoa include* Scaevola *'New Wonder' or wax begonias.*

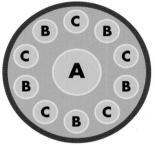

A Gentle Welcome

SUN PREFERENCE	CONTAINER SIZE	DIFFICULTY LEVEL
Partial Sun	Large	Easy

Shopping List

- Container mix potting soil
- 1 3-gallon-sized diplandenia (*Mandevilla splendens* 'Red Riding Hood') **A**
- 3 1-gallon-sized foxtail ferns (*Asparagus densiflorus* 'Myers') **B**
- 6 lantanas (*Lantana camara* 'New Gold') **C**
- 6 calibrachoas (*Calibrachoa* hybrid 'Cabernet Cherry Rose') **D**

This recipe may look sweet and delicate but it will take on a full day of summer sunshine in most environments. When you use this recipe where the summer days are regularly in the upper 90s, you will want to substitute the calibrachoa with *Purslane* or place this planter where it will be protected from the mid- to late afternoon sun.

Fill your container with container mix potting mix, leaving about 8 inches from the rim of the planter to the top of the soil. Place the diplandenia in the middle of the planter and look to see that the top of its rootball is about one inch below the level of the container's rim. Add enough soil around the rootball so the tops of the foxtail ferns' rootballs are level with the diplandenia. Add enough potting mix loosely around these plants until all the mix is about one inch below the rim of the planter, then plant the remaining plants according to recipe diagram.

Sometimes this diplandenia can only be found sold in nurseries trained on a trellis rather that the bush form seen here. You can choose to keep it on the trellis, which will give it a more formal look, or you can carefully remove the branches from the trellis and prune it to a bush form. These branches do tend to break easily after they have been on the trellis so proceed cautiously and expect to lose a few branches along the way. There is an interesting aspect to the 'Red Riding Hood' variety of diplandenia— the hotter the temperatures, the deeper pink the flower becomes until it almost looks red. This deeper color also showcases its golden throat; this is echoed in this recipe by the *Lantana* 'New Gold'. Care for this planter involves a monthly feeding of bloom-boosting fertilizer and watering when the top of the soil is dry to the touch.

PLANT OPTIONS

Where diplandenia is difficult to locate, try using Pentas *'Butterfly® Deep Rose.'* Helenium amarum *'Dakota Gold' is a good substitute for the lantana in this recipe.*

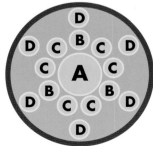

Grape & Orange Creamsickle

SUN PREFERENCE	CONTAINER SIZE	DIFFICULTY LEVEL
Partial Sun	Medium	Easy

Shopping List

- Container mix potting soil
- 1 1-gallon-sized variegated flax lily (*Dianella tasmanica* 'Variegata') **A**
- 3 begonias (*Begonia boliviensis* 'Bonfire™') **B**
- 2 coleus (*Solenostemon* 'Mint Mocha') **C**
- 3 coleus (*Solenostemon* 'Alamaba Sunset') **D**
- 1 verbena (*Verbena* 'Homestead Purple') **E**
- 2 variegated ivies (*Hedera* helix 'Glacier') **F**

Even though the plant companies introduce a hundred or so new cultivars every year to tempt us—and I am a little obsessive about trying out *all* the new plants—there are usually only a few that I will eagerly seek out the following year. *Begonia* 'Bonfire' is a plant that I keep on my "favorites" list and keep finding new ways to use it. This recipe pairs 'Bonfire' with another one of my favorite part sun plants, *Dianella tasmanica* 'Variegata', and with a couple of great coleus varieties for a delicious display of color. I also love how the glazed blue planter complements this recipe so well. The flax lily has a delicate blue flower that seems almost to reflect the blue hue of the planter.

Since the *Dianella* is both the centerpiece and the largest plant in the container, let this be the first plant placed in the container that you have already filled three-fourths with container mix potting soil. After planting the *Dianella*, pour in more soil if needed to bring the soil level to within two to three inches from the top of the planter. Position the coleus and begonias next, remembering that these plants grow very quickly and will not look as lush when they're first planted as they do in the picture shown here. Next, add the verbena and ivies, and then add more potting mix if needed to fill in spaces between the plants' roots.

Water the plants in this recipe when the top *three* to *four* inches of soil are dry to the touch. If you see the coleus or verbena leaves drooping or curling then you know it is time to water. *Begonia* 'Bonfire' will rot if the soil is kept too moist, so err on the side of underwatering since the coleus and verbena will let you know when it is time to water. Fertilize once a month with a general-purpose plant food.

PLANT OPTIONS

Substitute Panicum *'Strawberries and Cream' if the* Dianella *is difficult to locate.* Calibrachoa *'Trailing Blue' could be used instead of the verbena.*

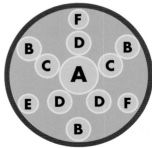

Hot Fudge Sundae

SUN PREFERENCE	CONTAINER SIZE	DIFFICULTY LEVEL
Partial Sun	Extra Large	Moderate

Shopping List

- Container mix potting soil
- 1 5-gallon-sized dracaena palm (*Cordyline australis* 'Southern Splendor') **A**
- 3 3-gallon-sized fringe flowers (*Loropetalum chinense* 'Suzanne') **B**
- 9 1-gallon-sized caladiums (*Caladium* 'White Wing') **C**
- 6 vincas (*Catharanthus roseus* 'Mediterranean XP Dark Red') **D**
- 7 sweet potato vines (*Ipomoea batatas* 'Blackie') **E**

Summertime doesn't quite seem the same for me without at least *one* hot fudge sundae with chocolate dripping down the sides of the bowl. This recipe is one huge bowl of yumminess—a visual treat for a summer day. In cooler climates where temperatures rarely reach above the upper 80s, this recipe will do just fine in full sun. But in summer areas warmer that zone 7, you'll want to protect the caladiums and *Loropetalum* from afternoon sun.

Fill your planter a little over halfway full of container mix potting soil and position the dracaena palm as indicated in the recipe diagram. Add more soil as needed so that when the *Loropetalum* is planted, the top of the rootball on the dracaena palm is level with the top of the *Loropetalum* rootballs. Repeat this same process of adding a little more soil to get this same level result with the caladium, followed by the vincas and sweet potato vines. Don't be concerned if the sweet potato vines look a little skimpy when first planted: like a good fudge sauce, they will start spilling down the sides as the summer heat rises.

Care for this container can be a little tricky in that the *Loropetalum* don't like to be forgotten when it comes to watering and are a little difficult to bring back to their former glory quickly if they do dry out. The trick here is to use the sweet potato vines as your indicator plants to show that this recipe is ready for a good, long drink of water—when 'Blackie' looks wilted, *quickly* water! Fertilize once a month with a general-purpose plant food.

PLANT OPTIONS

*Use red ivy geraniums rather than vinca in cooler climates. Purple
fountain grass, Pennisetum 'Rubrum', would be a suitable substitute
for the dracaena palm.*

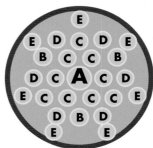

Hot Summer Fun

SUN PREFERENCE	CONTAINER SIZE	DIFFICULTY LEVEL
Full Sun	**Extra Large**	**Easy**

Shopping List

- Container mix potting soil
- 1 3-gallon-sized red oleander (*Nerium oleander*) **A**
- 1 2-gallon-sized yellow allamanda bush (*Allamanda*) **B**
- 1 2-gallon-sized mandevilla (*Mandevilla* hybrid 'Sun Parasol® Crimson') **C**
- 3 1-gallon-sized asparagus ferns (*Asparagus setaceus*) **D**
- 2 lantanas (*Lantana* 'New Gold') **E**

Find the hottest, sunniest spot in your garden and let this recipe keep the summer beauty flowing. Filled with plants that bloom *more* the hotter it gets, this is also a very good combination for those who want big punch of color but don't have time for a lot of maintenance. In cooler climates, the oleander, mandevilla, and allamanda bush need to have some mature growth on them in order to produce the number of flowers needed for that *wow* factor; that is why I recommend buying two- and three-gallon-sized plants. But this also makes this recipe a good one to choose for those extra-large planters that can be so hard to fill up.

For this planting I recommend placing the oleander first in your planter that has been partially filled with container mix potting soil. (Oleander can be poisonous or irritating to the skin so I *highly* recommend wearing gloves and long sleeves when planting. You will also want to look at plant options for the oleander if you have a pet that likes to nibble on your plants or even dig in your pots.) Add a little more soil around the rootball before adding the next ingredients. Next, you will want to shave a little off the rootball of both the mandevilla and the allamanda when you place them in the planter, tilting them slightly to the outside of the container. Place the asparagus ferns in the container as directed by the recipe diagram, then add the lantanas.

The lantanas will become established during the first few weeks after planting so observe them closely for watering needs (the leaves droop when thirsty). I usually allow the top *four* or *five* inches of soil to dry out on this recipe before watering. If you see the leaves on the mandevilla and the allamanda start to turn yellow, and the soil does not seem very dry, you need to water less. A monthly feeding of bloom-boosting fertilizer will help keep the flowers flowing throughout the summertime.

PLANT OPTIONS

Try using a Knock Out® rose instead of the oleander and Rudbeckia *'Indian Summer' as a substitute for the allamanda.*

The Hot Tropics

SUN PREFERENCE	CONTAINER SIZE	DIFFICULTY LEVEL
Partial Sun	Large	Easy

Shopping List

- Container mix potting soil
- 1 3-gallon-sized banana tree (*Musa acuminata* 'Zebrina') **A**
- 5 chenille plants (*Acalypha hispida* 'Firetail') **B**
- 4 coleus (*Solenostemon* 'Florida Sun Jade') **C**
- 3 bleeding heart vines (*Clerodendrum* 'Red') **D**

Few plants can command as much attention simply with their foliage as a banana tree does, especially *Musa acuminata* 'Zebrina', which has a burgundy red splash of color decorating its leaves. With the potential to reach six to eight feet height in most growing regions, this banana tree can easily make a bold statement all on its own. But underscore that with a few complementary plants and you might have folks stopping by just to check out your container planting! The mixture of the heavy banana leaves, the cut foliage of the coleus, the funny fuzzy chenille flowers, and the wiry bleeding heart vines create a collage of foliage textures and subtle colors.

Since the banana tree is planted in the center of the container and is the largest plant in the container, you will want to get this securely planted before adding the remaining plants. Depending on how deep your planter is, add enough container mix potting soil so that the 3-gallon-sized banana tree can sit deep enough in the planter where the top of its rootball is at least one inch below the top of the container. Fill in with potting soil around the rootball, making sure that the banana tree is not leaning. Finish planting the remaining plants according to the recipe diagram.

Keep the soil evenly moist in this recipe by watering when the top of the soil is dry to your touch. To maintain a tidy appearance throughout the season, cut back any banana leaves that are looking faded or torn by the wind. With pruning shears, cut the leaves at the base of the leaf where it is growing from the stalk. Pinch off the flowers of the coleus for the first two months of growth to encourage the coleus to branch and fill out. In late summer, allow the coleus to bloom and enjoy the thick show of blue flower spikes. Fertilize monthly with a bloom-boosting plant food.

PLANT OPTIONS

Think of using Colocasia antiquorum *'Illustris'*, Alocasia *'Hilo Beauty'*, or Canna *'Tropicana™ Black'* *rather than the banana tree in this recipe.*

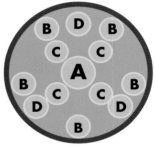

Hummingbird Magnet

SUN PREFERENCE	CONTAINER SIZE	DIFFICULTY LEVEL
Full Sun	Large	Easy

Shopping List

- Container mix potting soil
- 1 3-gallon-sized tropical hibiscus (*Hibiscus rosa-sinensis* 'Hula Girl') **A**
- 5 1-gallon-sized bougainvilleas (*Bougainvillea* 'Purple Queen®') **B**
- 5 ivy geraniums (*Pelargonium peltatum* 'Calliope™ Dark Red') **C**

Place this recipe out in a sunny spot and it usually won't be long until the hummingbirds come to visit. Relatively easy to care for, these three different types of plants keep a big display of color coming all summer long. Hibiscus flowers open during the day and often close up at night so choose a spot where this recipe will be seen most often during the daytime hours.

Start putting this container recipe together by filling your planter halfway with container mix potting soil. Before placing the hibiscus in the center of the planter, loosen the soil around its rootball to encourage the roots to spread throughout the container. I have noticed that the larger the size of the hibiscus, the more likely it is to be rootbound, so this root loosening process is important for a healthier container planting. After planting the hibiscus, add a little more potting mix around the hibiscus roots before planting the bougainvilleas. The geraniums can be placed next, adding more soil if needed to cover all the roots in the container.

Some folks can get a little frustrated with bougainvilleas because they tend to bloom like crazy, then rest, but they do not always give a consistent summertime display. Bougainvilleas perform best if they're kept a little on the dry side and are well fed with a bloom-boosting plant fertilizer. It is actually better to wait until the hibiscus leaves are just starting to droop a little from thirst before you water it again. By keeping all these plants slightly on the thirsty side, more blooms will be produced. Pinch off the faded heads of the geraniums throughout the summer and clean up any fallen hibiscus flowers to maintain a clean look.

PLANT OPTIONS

You can use the same genus of plants but different cultivars to create a great new look. Try using Hibiscus *'The President',* Bougainvillea *'Raspberry Ice', and an ivy geranium such as* Pelargonium *'Blizzard Blue'.*

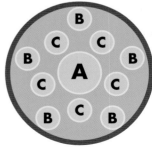

Invite Me to Come

SUN PREFERENCE
Full Sun

CONTAINER SIZE
Small

DIFFICULTY LEVEL
Easy

Shopping List

- Container mix potting soil
- 1 1-gallon-sized mandevilla (*Mandevilla* hybrid 'Sun Parasol Crimson') **A**
- 2 petunias (*Petunia* hybrid 'Royal Velvet') **B**
- 2 verbenas (*Verbena* hybrid 'Babylon Red') **C**
- 2 licorice vines (*Helichrysum* 'Limelight') **D**
- 1 golden creeping jenny (*Lysimachia aurea*) **E**

Like a good quality classic shirt or dress that can be adapted to different styles by simply changing a few accessories, a good quality classic plant can become the basis for building a wide variety of plantings. My "go to" plant for summer annuals is *Mandevilla* 'Sun Parasol Crimson'. This plant is drought tolerant, has smaller leaves than the traditional mandevilla (whose large leaves can sometimes smother more delicate underplantings), and it can be pruned to a more bushy form. I also find that it will continue to bloom faithfully in part sun condition. 'Sun Parasol' also comes in 'Giant Crimson', 'Burgundy', 'White', and 'Pink'. When a client tells me they want lots of color but low maintenance, this plant is usually where I start.

This recipe combines a group of easy care plants while giving a burst of welcoming color. Mixing flowering plants with interesting foliage plants like *Lysimachia aurea* and *Helichrysum* 'Limelight' give a container recipe color and diverse texture.

When choosing a smaller planter in a full sun location, stay away from using black or dark colored planters, especially if they are iron or another metal. These will heat up the soil quickly and many plants' root systems will cook in that type environment. In this recipe, plant the mandevilla first in the loosely poured potting mix in the container. Add more soil around the rootball if needed before adding the remaining plants. After all is planted there should be about one inch from the rim of the planter to the top of the soil. All the varieties in this recipe are happy in full sun, although the *Lysimachia* will perform best if the container is turned so that this plant is facing north or east to avoid getting the full blast of afternoon sun.

Water when the top of the soil feels dry to the touch and fertilize monthly with bloom-boosting fertilizer. The *Lysimachia aurea* and *Helichrysum* 'Limelight' can both get very long in a summer's growth so trim back halfway down the container in the midsummer to keep your container from looking like Rapunzel.

PLANT OPTIONS

Instead of the Helichrysum *'Limelight,' another plant to try would be* Lotus *'Amazon Sunset'. You'll be happy with either one of those.*

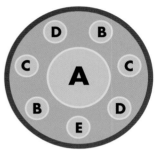

Look At Me!

SUN PREFERENCE	CONTAINER SIZE	DIFFICULTY LEVEL
Full Sun	Extra Large	Moderate

Shopping List

- Container mix potting soil
- 1 extra-large strawberry jar planter
- 1 3-gallon-sized bush allamanda (*Allamanda nerifolia* 'Yellow') **A**
- 3 purple queen (*Setcresea*) **B**
- 3 geraniums (*Pelargonium* 'Contessa Red') **C**
- 5 purslanes (*Portulaca oleracea* 'Rio Scarlet') **D**
- 5 purslanes (*Portulaca oleracea* 'Rio Yellow') **E**

Not all container recipes have had the same impact that this one keeps having. And all this impact is caused by such low maintenance plants! The key to helping plants survive in a strawberry jar is to use succulent type plants in the strawberry jar "cups." In this recipe I used purslanes in the cups, and they seemed to be quite happy.

Planting this container is not as tricky as it looks. Place the 4-inch purslanes in the cups of the strawberry jar before pouring in the container mix potting soil. This will help prevent soil from seeping out of the cups while it is being poured into the planter. Leave enough room at the top of the planter to plant the 3-gallon-sized allamanda and remaining annuals according to the recipe diagram. Add any soil mix that is needed to fill in any gaps around the planted allamanda, geraniums, and purple queen. Also, fill in any gaps that remain in the cups holding the purslanes.

Keep this recipe on the dry side for these sun-loving plants. Stick your finger about 3 inches into the dirt and if you feel any moisture, wait another day before watering again. These extra-large and large planters, when watered properly by saturating the soil, will allow you to go longer times between watering once the plantings get established (which usually takes 2 to 3 weeks during the summer). Even though these plants all need less water than many other annuals, they still need a monthly feeding of bloom-boosting fertilizer. The only other maintenance needed besides watering and fertilizing is to pinch back the stems of the old geranium flowers that are past looking good.

PLANT OPTIONS

For those who live in cooler climates, don't worry if you can't locate the bush allamanda. Swap out the allamanda by using Hemerocallis *'Happy Returns' daylily for a similar trumpet flower or use* Lantana *'Landmark® Yellow' to simply keep the yellow color.*

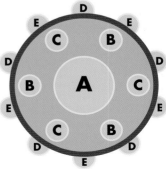

Majesty

SUN PREFERENCE	CONTAINER SIZE	DIFFICULTY LEVEL
Full Sun	**Medium**	**Easy**

Shopping List

- **Container mix potting soil**
- **3 summer snapdragons** (*Angelonia* 'Angelface Purple') **A**
- **3 petunias** (*Petunia* hybrid 'Royal Velvet') **B**
- **3 petunias** (*Petunia* hybrid 'Royal Magenta') **C**
- **2 calibrachoas** (*Calibrachoa* 'Superbells Yellow') **D**

One of the first projects I had when I started planting containers as a professional was designing and planting hundreds of containers like the one in this recipe. Few plantings could be as simple as placing eleven 4-inch plants in a rectangular planter, yet few things have had the summer-long impact that these annual plantings have had on the neighborhoods where my clients live. I learned early on that high quality plants result in high quality products for my clients. That is a difference that you will find in deck box plantings like the one in this picture, a planting that lasted from mid-April until mid-October. So what is the lesson to be learned here? Start with good quality even in the little things, like the choice you make in a 4-inch-sized plant and the soil you plant it in.

Fill the deck box with container mix potting soil, leaving one inch of space between the top of the soil and the rim of the deck box. Plant the annuals listed in the recipe following the recipe diagram. You will notice immediately that the deck box that you've just planted does not look like the one in the picture. Another lesson that I've learned is that summer container annuals perform best when they start small and are given the opportunity to establish themselves in the environment where they will grow all summer. So what is the second lesson learned in this recipe planting? Patience is a virtue and good things come to those who wait. Give this planting a couple of weeks to grow together and you'll never go back to cramming hanging baskets bought at the grocery store into a planter to get instant gratification.

In a summer planting like this with so many flowering plants, daily watering is usually a *must*, especially during the first two weeks of establishing the roots. If the planting still feels moist on the soil surface, wait another day before watering. Fertilize once a month with a bloom-boosting fertilizer. By choosing higher quality plants to start with, the plants in this recipe do not need the pruning and pinching back that other plant varieties will need.

PLANT OPTIONS

By taking out the yellow calibrachoas and using Scaevola 'New Wonder' instead, you can create a cool color palette that is both striking and inviting during the summer months.

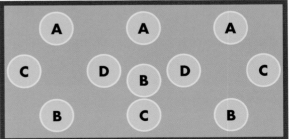

Mandevilla Explosion

SUN PREFERENCE	CONTAINER SIZE	DIFFICULTY LEVEL
Full Sun	Extra Large	Intermediate

Shopping List

- Container mix potting soil
- 1 5-gallon-sized trellised white mandevilla vine (*Mandevilla*) **A**
- 3 2-gallon-sized New Zealand flax (*Phormium* 'Rainbow Chief') **B**
- 3 2-gallon-sized spireas (*Spirea japonica* 'Goldmound') **C**
- 3 1-gallon-sized caladiums (*Caladium* 'Pink Beauty') **D**
- 3 coleus (*Solenostemon* 'Solar Shadow') **E**
- 3 petunias (*Petunia* hybrid 'Royal Velvet') **F**
- 3 cupheas (*Cuphea llavea* 'Totally Tempted') **G**

If you are looking for a container recipe that erupts with color during the day but also will draw your eye in the evening, this combination may be just what you need. Another one of my co-worker Yelena's masterful creations, I love how—even though she used several plants similar to what is used in Spiky Color Burst— she designed a look with colors and appeal quite different from that one.

The centerpiece of this recipe is the white trellised mandevilla vine, which will need to be planted first in the container. Depending on the depth of your planter, you may need to add enough potting mix in your planter so that when placed in position, the top of the rootball on the mandevilla vine will be about one inch below the rim of the container. Keep the vine on the trellis for the look desired in this recipe. Add more of the container mix potting soil to keep

the mandevilla upright, also adding the spireas and *Phormium* to keep this trellised vine in position. Follow up with the caladiums and coleus, adding the cupheas and petunias as your final touch. Finish by filling in any spaces between the rootballs with more soil.

To maintain this sun-loving container recipe, water when the top two inches of the soil is dry to the touch. The mandevilla leaves will start to turn yellow if overwatered so if you notice this, check to see if the soil is not being allowed a chance to dry out between watering, and adjust your watering schedule. Fertilize monthly with a general-purpose fertilizer. As hard as it sounds, you should pinch off the pretty blue flower spikes on the coleus for the first couple of months in the summer to encourage them to become fuller. Depending on how long your growing season is, you may want to pinch back the petunias if they start looking too spindly.

PLANT OPTIONS

Substitute a red ivy geranium if the cuphea is hard to locate. Pennisetum *'Princess Molly' would make an interesting alternative to the* Phormium.

Oh, So Easy

SUN PREFERENCE	CONTAINER SIZE	DIFFICULTY LEVEL
Full Sun	Large	Moderate

Shopping List

- Container mix potting soil
- 1 5-gallon-sized mandevilla vine (*Mandevilla amabilis* 'Crimson Jewel') **A**
- 5 cupheas (*Cuphea llavea* 'Flamenco Samba') **B**
- 5 bidens (*Bidens ferulifolia* 'Peter's Gold Carpet') **C**

One of the challenges of summer color is finding a vine that blooms all season long that can also handle the drought that sometimes accompanies the summer months. Mandevilla vine is one of my favorite "foolproof" vines for summer containers. Whether you keep this on the nursery-provided bamboo stakes or provide a decorative obelisk to train the vine branches on, the mandevilla gives impact with fast growing and constantly blooming performance.

This container recipe is a combination of three of my favorite summer sun-loving annuals. Once the root system is established for this container combination, which usually takes three or four weeks, this recipe is one of the easy care plantings. Medium to low water needs, fertilizing with a bloom-boosting plant food once a month, and no need for pinching back blooms—all this is what gives this recipe its name of Oh, So Easy.

If you are wondering why a recipe titled Oh, So Easy can have a difficulty level of moderate,

the slight inconsistency comes in the planting process. As much as I love the simple care needs of the mandevilla, planting a large and already trellised mandevilla vine can be a little tricky. Leave the vines on the stakes and plant this vine in the container before planting any of the other plant ingredients. A few of the branches of the mandevilla may break off while planting so gently remove any damaged vines. If you are going to add your own obelisk in the container, use one that will fit over the staked vine. Then remove any tape or strings that are holding the vine branches to the stakes and holding the stakes together. Gently pull the stakes upward, twisting them as needed to loosen the vines, then wrapping the loosened vines around the poles of the obelisk.

After situating the mandevilla in the container, continue adding the remaining ingredients. If you see any yellowing in the mandevilla leaves you'll know you are most likely watering too much.

PLANT OPTIONS

Pandorea jasminoides *'Charisma' bower vine is a little more flamboyant with its variegated foliage, but less prolific in blooms if you need a substitution for the mandevilla. Another vine substitution to maintain the red center-plant coloring would be to use red passionflower,* Passiflora racemosa.

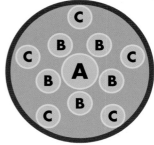

Peek-a-Boo Punch

SUN PREFERENCE	CONTAINER SIZE	DIFFICULTY LEVEL
Full Sun	**Large**	**Easy**

Shopping List

- **Container mix potting soil**
- **1 5-gallon-sized New Zealand flax (*Phormium* 'Sundowner') A**
- **5 spilanthes (*Spilanthes oleracea* 'Peek A Boo') B**
- **5 verbenas (*Verbena* 'Lanai™ Peach') C**

When I first designed this recipe, several of my co-workers thought it was *way* too boring. But imagine how this container would look to a young child who is running around playing, and she suddenly turns to find a whole bunch of little brown eyes staring at her! I enjoy having a display with softer, muted colors and I like the echo of yellow between the spilanthes and *Phormium*, and the echoing peach shades between the *Phormium* and verbenas.

After filling your container about two-thirds full of container mix potting soil, position the New Zealand flax in the center of the planter. You will want to make sure that the top of the rootball on the *Phormium* is about one inch lower than the edge of the planter so you may have to make an indention in the soil so that the plant sits lower in the pot. After positioning this plant correctly, add enough potting mix to finish

filling the planter, leaving about 3 inches of space from the top of the soil to the container's rim. This should give you enough space to place the remaining plants. After placing the spilanthes and verbenas, add any additional soil necessary to fill in the spaces between these smaller plants.

Little attention is needed for maintaining this container recipe. Water only when the top two inches of soil feels dry to touch. The verbenas are good indicator plants for watering needs—their leaves will start to curl and droop when underwatered. Once or twice throughout the summer you may want to cut off the old blooms of the verbenas. Fertilize once a month with a bloom-boosting plant food. A fringe benefit of this recipe is that the spilanthes flower heads make an interesting addition to cut flower arrangements.

PLANT OPTIONS

Pennisetum *'Fireworks'*
could be substituted
for the Phormium.

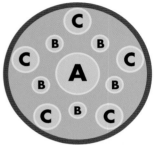

Peppermint Candy

SUN PREFERENCE
Full Sun

CONTAINER SIZE
Extra Large

DIFFICULTY LEVEL
Intermediate

Shopping List

- Container mix potting soil
- 1 7-gallon-sized purple peppermint tree (*Agonis flexuosa* 'After Dark') **A**
- 7 1-gallon-sized mandevilla vines (*Mandevilla* 'Sun Parasol Crimson') **B**
- 7 geraniums (*Pelargonium* 'Freestyle Ruby Red') **C**
- 5 6-inch variegated society garlic plants (*Tulbaghia violacea*) **D**

Don't let the "Intermediate" level of this planting scare you away—what makes this planting difficult is that you are dealing with a large, bulky plant and an extra-large container, which may require an extra pair of hands to assist in planting. I'll also let you know that I killed three *Agonis* trees before I realized that they *really* like to stay away from being overwatered. This recipe combines a group of plants that all thrive in slightly dry soil so hopefully you will have no temptation to overwater.

One of the ongoing debates I hear in the container gardening circles is whether to add something besides potting mix to the bottoms of large containers to reduce some of the expense of the potting soil. (For a large or extra-large container, you could use a lot of potting mix.) Personally, I like to encourage every plant to send its roots as *deeply* as possible into the container. Therefore, rather than using an inorganic material, the only product that I may fill the bottom one-fourth of a planter with is pine

mulch or shredded hardwood mulch. Both of these will break down into finer organic material.

The first plant to place in this container will be the *Agonis*. It helps to have someone hold the tree straight while you stand back to make sure that the tree is not leaning one way or the other. Fill in potting mix around the rootball, leaving enough space to add the remaining ingredients around the rootball. Plant the mandevilla plants next, then step back to make sure the tree has not started tilting with the planting activity going on around it. Finish by planting the remaining ingredients according the recipe diagram.

These large and extra-large containers have the advantage of holding more water and often do not need to be watered as often once the plants get established, which usually takes three to four weeks for these annuals. This is a recipe that calls for plants that have low water requirements so water well, then allow the top *3 to 4 inches* to dry out before watering again. Fertilize each month with a bloom-boosting plant food.

PLANT OPTIONS

Don't get discouraged if you have a hard time finding this cool peppermint tree. A few options that will provide a very similar look would be Black Lace™ elderberry, Sambucus nigra *'Eva',* or ninebark, Physocarpus opulifolious *'Summer Wine®'.*

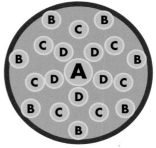

Perfection

SUN PREFERENCE	CONTAINER SIZE	DIFFICULTY LEVEL
Partial Sun	**Medium**	**Easy**

Shopping List

- Container mix potting soil
- 1 1-gallon-sized elephant ear (*Colocasia* 'Red Stem') **A**
- 1 Persian shield (*Strobilanthes*) **B**
- 1 silver sage (*Salvia argentea* 'Silver Sage') **C**
- 1 zebrina wandering Jew (*Tradescantia zebrina*) **D**
- 1 artemisia (*Artemisia aborescens* 'Powis Castle') **E**
- 3 petunias (*Petunia* hybrid 'Supertunia® Mini Silver') **F**

The French philosopher Voltaire said, "Perfection is attained by slow degrees; it requires the hand of time." A container garden, or any garden for that matter, may seem to reach perfection at different degrees of growth, only to reveal that the next degree is even more perfect. When I saw this part sun container recipe, I thought that this combination was close to perfection. Color echoes of purple are reflected in the Persian shield, the stem of the *Colocasia*, in the wandering Jew, and in the throat of the petunia. Silver and white tones are seen in the wandering Jew, the petunia, the artemisia, the salvia, and the Persian shield. Huge leaves from the *Colocasia* and *Salvia* contrast *beautifully* with the finely cut foliage of the artemisia.

Since the elephant ear is the largest plant and the focal point of your planting, plant it first in your container that you have filled with container mix potting soil. Place the artemisia next, planting it at a slight angle toward the outside of the container. Add the *Strobilanthes*, sage, and zebrina wandering Jew as demonstrated by the recipe diagram, followed by the petunias. This variety of petunia, 'Mini Silver', seems to bloom just fine in partial sun without growing too leggy.

Water this container when the top two inches of soil are dry to your touch and fertilize with a general-purpose fertilizer once a month. Prune the petunias in midsummer to keep blooms coming all along the plant stems. In climates cooler than zone 5, this recipe could be used as a sun planting but you may want to make sure that the Persian shield and the wandering Jew are not facing the harsher afternoon sun. The *Colocasia* will keep them somewhat shaded, but they still will be happiest with having only the morning sun exposure.

PLANT OPTIONS

It is hard to mess with perfection, but if you have to substitute something for the sage, use lamb's ear, Stachys byzantina.

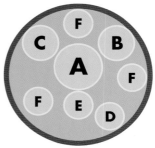

Pretty Thing

SUN PREFERENCE	CONTAINER SIZE	DIFFICULTY LEVEL
Full Sun	Large	Easy

Shopping List

- Container mix potting soil
- 3 pentas (*Pentas* 'Butterfly Red') **A**
- 3 fan flowers (*Scaevola* 'New Wonder®') **B**
- 3 bidens (*Bidens* 'Peter's Gold Carpet') **C**
- 3 iresine (*Iresine* 'Purple Lady') **D**

One of my favorite places to visit when I am in the Panhandle of Florida is a section called Highway 30A. Along this 18-mile strip are lovely little beachside villages, many of them with beautiful container plantings scattered throughout their community areas. This recipe is one that I saw in Seaside, Florida, where the movie *The Truman Show* was filmed. The rich contrast of dark foliage and bright flowers was striking in its simplicity.

All of the plants in this sun-loving recipe are fast growing and can fill up a container quickly. I have suggested a large container but if you are longing for more instant gratification, either use a medium-sized planter or spend a little more money on larger plants. In my experience, after about four weeks of proper care, it will be hard to tell whether you used 4-inch-sized plants or gallon-sized plants—the little guys catch up. First, fill the planter to within three inches from the rim with container mix potting soil. Plant the pentas as shown in the recipe diagram, adding the *Scaevola*, *Bidens*, and iresine in consecutive order. Add any extra potting mix if needed to cover the roots of the plants. Be forewarned: it may look a little skimpy when first planted.

One of the specific qualities that make this container planting so desirable is that it needs no pruning when properly watered and fertilized. Water only when the top two inches of soil are dry to touch. Feed this planting every other week with a bloom-boosting fertilizer that has been diluted to half the strength of what would normally be used. Another benefit is that the pentas and the iresine make a nice addition to cut flower arrangements.

PLANT OPTIONS

*Trailing coleus 'Wedding Veil' or other trailing coleus cultivars can be
used instead of iresine in this recipe.*

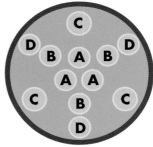

Riot of Color

SUN PREFERENCE	CONTAINER SIZE	DIFFICULTY LEVEL
Full Sun	Large	Intermediate

Shopping List

- Container mix potting soil
- 1 1-gallon-sized variegated grass (*Phalaris arundinacea* 'Strawberries and Cream') **A**
- 1 1-quart-sized euphorbia (*Euphorbia characias* 'Tasmanian Tiger') **B**
- 1 1-gallon-sized agave (*Agave* hybrid) **C**
- 2 sedums (*Sedum repestre* 'Angelina') **D**
- 2 spilanthes (*Spilanthes oleracea* 'Peek-A-Boo') **E**
- 2 petunias (*Petunia* hybrid 'Royal Magenta') **F**
- 2 calibrachoas (*Calibrachoa* 'Apricot Punch') **G**
- 2 verbenas (*Verbena* hybrid 'Superbena® Burgundy') **H**
- 2 ivy geraniums (*Pelargonium* 'Taj Mahal') **I**

Yes, this recipe is just what it sounds like—a little of this and a little of that. Throw it all together in a large planter and bake it in the sun for the summer for a yummy collection of color and textures all season long. The contrasts in foliage between the thin blades of grass, the thick agave leaves, the delicate oval leaves of the euphorbia, and the other flowering plant foliage keep the planting interesting. At the same time the echoes of color found among the recipe's cream, burgundy, and apricot shades give the combination a continuity and cohesiveness.

After filling your planter about halfway with container mix potting soil, place the three one-gallon-sized plants as shown by the recipe diagram. I may sound a little like the overprotective mother here when I say this, but I recommend either wearing glasses, sunglasses, or safety glasses whenever you are handling agaves, plus wearing gloves and long-sleeved shirts. Normally, I would suggest planting this last in a container but since the agave is larger than the remaining ingredients, planting it later may disrupt what you've already placed. After you have these three plants in place, add the geraniums and verbenas, then place the remaining ingredients following the recipe diagram. Add potting mix if needed to cover any open areas between the roots of the plants.

A container crammed this full of plants will end up with a lot of roots and less soil so keep an eye on this planting to observe anything that may look like it is starting to wilt. Water when the top two inches of soil are dry, and feed monthly with a general-purpose fertilizer. Every two weeks, pinch off the faded geranium and verbena blossoms.

PLANT OPTIONS

For a softer alternative to the agave, use hens and chicks Sempervivum *'Green Wheel'.*

Royal Purple

SUN PREFERENCE	CONTAINER SIZE	DIFFICULTY LEVEL
Partial Sun	Medium	Easy

Shopping List

- Container mix potting soil
- 1 3-gallon-sized purple grass (*Pennisetum purpureum* 'Princess') **A**
- 3 begonias (*Begonia* 'Dragonwing® Red') **B**
- 3 variegated ivies (*Hedera helix* 'Gold Child') **C**

It doesn't get much easier than this when it comes to part sun summer plantings. While I won't go so far as to say that you can plant this and forget about it, you can plant this and, after it has rooted in for a few weeks, forget about it for several days and not worry about coming home to dead plants. If you live in extremely hot areas, you may be able to only skip one day so take your heat zone into consideration with this instruction. All three of these plants thrive in low water environments. In fact, I've seen more *Pennisetum*, Dragonwing® begonias, and ivy killed from *overwatering* than I have ever seen from underwatering.

Fill your medium-sized planter halfway with container mix potting soil, then position the purple grass in the center of your container. Add more soil to stabilize the grass and raise the planting level of the soil for the remaining plants.

Plant the begonias, tilting them slightly toward the *outside* edge of the container, then finish by adding the ivies as shown in the recipe diagram. Begonias can be a little fragile when you are planting them so don't be too concerned if a few stems are broken off in the planting process—they will quickly be replaced by new growth.

As mentioned, maintenance of this recipe is extremely easy. Water only when the top three to four inches of soil feel dry to your touch. One way that you can tell if you are overwatering is that the begonias will become limp or even mushy. Fertilize once a month with a general-purpose plant food. The blades of the *Pennisetum* 'Princess' are nice to use to line or swirl inside a vase of cut flowers. With this recipe, feel free to take off for a summer weekend and have a healthy container planting to welcome you back home!

PLANT OPTIONS

Cordyline *'Cabernett'*
is a good substitute for
Pennisetum *'Princess'* grass.
Plectranthus *'Variegata'* can
be used as an alternative to
the ivies.

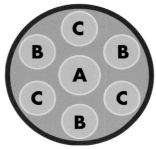

Shady Summer Surprises

SUN PREFERENCE	CONTAINER SIZE	DIFFICULTY LEVEL
Shade	Small	Easy

Shopping List

- Container mix potting soil
- 2 1-quart-sized cannas (*Canna* hybrid 'Pink Sunburst') **A**
- 1 begonia (*Begonia* 'Dragonwing® Pink') **B**
- 1 variegated sedge grass (*Carex phyllocephala* 'Sparkler') **C**
- 2 mini hostas (*Hosta* 'Mighty Mouse') **D**
- 1 bugleweed (*Ajuga reptans* 'Bronze Beauty') **E**
- 2 variegated ivies (*Hedera helix* 'Gold Child') **F**

Shady spots are sometimes overlooked in their potential for creating truly artistic displays. The potential for using certain non-shade plants like this miniature canna broadens the spectrum of plants you can choose from. Shady Summer Surprises is an interesting assortment of texture and foliage that offers some surprises throughout the summer. In zone 5 areas and cooler, placing this container in a part sun area will allow the canna to bloom, but in warmer areas the canna will be used solely for foliage.

Fill your window box or planter halfway with container mix potting soil, then position the cannas as shown in the recipe diagram. Next, add the begonia and *Carex*. Begonias can break easily when they're planted so handle them *gently* as you place them in the planter. If you break off a few branches, don't be too concerned because they do grow quickly. Next, as you plant the hostas,

position them tilting a little away from the begonia and *Carex*. When the hostas bloom (one of the fun summer surprises in this recipe), their flowers will provide a wider display at this angle. The ivies can be placed next; pull any long stems gently through the other foliage to develop a mingled look among the foliage. The bugleweed will be planted last, once again tilting the plant toward the front of the planter to encourage it spill over the edge of the planter. Finally, fill in with soil between any of the spaces left between the rootballs.

This recipe is very easy to care for with the biggest concern being not to overwater it! Test the soil moisture by sticking a finger at least two inches into the soil; only water when this test confirms that the soil is dry. The begonia will start to turn yellow and drop leaves if it is getting too much water. Feed this recipe once a month with a general-purpose fertilizer.

PLANT OPTIONS

If the canna is difficult to locate, try using one of the smaller, dark colored Alocasia *varieties like 'African Mask'.* Plectranthus *'Variegata' could be substituted for the hostas.*

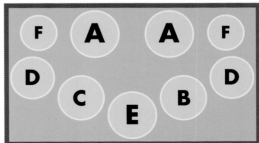

Shrimp Cocktail

SUN PREFERENCE	CONTAINER SIZE	DIFFICULTY LEVEL
Full Sun	Small	Easy

Shopping List

- Container mix potting soil
- 1 1-gallon-sized yellow shrimp plant (*Pachystachys lutea*) **A**
- 2 annual vincas (*Vinca* 'Pacifica XP Cherry Red') **B**
- 2 annual (*really* red) vincas (*Vinca* 'Pacifica XP Really Red') **C**
- 2 lantanas (*Lantana* 'Landmark Yellow') **D**
- 1 variegated Bermuda grass (*Cynodon dactylon* 'Burmuda Ghost') **E**
- 1 red petunia (*Petunia* hybrid) **F**
- 1 globe amaranth (*Gomphrena* 'Gnome Purple') **G**
- 1 euphorbia (*Euphorbia graminea* 'Diamond Frost') **H**

I have found that some plants seem to elicit a polarizing reaction. Folks tend either to love or hold particular plants in disdain, particularly ones with flowers that could be described as "artsy." This container recipe holds three plants that fit in the either love/hate category. The shrimp plant is one that a co-worker of mine will roll her eyes at. She thinks they look creepy but I think they add great vertical appeal and wonderful color. The other two controversial plants are the variegated Bermuda grass (mention Bermuda to some people and they immediately start mixing Round-Up™ herbicide) and globe amaranth (a reliable, old-fashioned annual; I still haven't figured out why it causes a mixed emotional response). But all of these plants are *great* ingredients in a creative, sun-loving container.

Using a small planter for this recipe gives a full look instantly. Only fill your container about three-fourths full of container mix potting soil and begin by positioning the shrimp plant as shown in the recipe diagram. Next, add the lantana and globe amaranth. Position the remaining plants at a slight angle toward the outer rim of the planter, encouraging each to spill over the edge.

All of these plants are happiest when kept a little on the dry side so avoid overwatering. If you see the shrimp plant or petunia leaves drooping, you'll know it's time to water. Pinch back the petunias several inches from their ends if you are only getting blossoms at the end of each branch. If lantana goes to seed, which can happen if you get periods of cool or very wet weather during the summer, cut these off so that the plant puts more energy in producing blooms. Fertilize monthly with a bloom-boosting plant food.

PLANT OPTIONS

If the shrimp plant is just too strange for your tastes, go with
Rudbeckia *'Tiger Eye'*.

So Elegant

SUN PREFERENCE	CONTAINER SIZE	DIFFICULTY LEVEL
Full Sun	Large	Easy

Shopping List

- Container mix potting soil
- 1 1-gallon-sized duranta (*Duranta erecta* 'Gold Edge') **A**
- 3 purple queen (*Setcresea*) **B**
- 3 verbenas (*Verbena* hybrid 'Homestead Purple') **C**
- 3 mandevillas (*Mandevilla* hybrid 'Sun Parasol Crimson') **D**

Every summer for the past few years, these planters have been one of my yearly challenges. Exposed to wind and full sun, they also are the focal point in one of the main entryways into a beautiful neighborhood. They are in front of large hollies and red Knock Out® roses, so I had to figure out not only what would stand out, but what would survive under those conditions.

Duranta 'Gold Edge', a plant that I had seen handle the winds and heat of Texas, worked well with its bright golden contrast in front of the green hollies. Red mandevilla and *Setcresea* are both faithful standouts for handling tough conditions, as is 'Homestead Purple' verbena once it gets established in a planting. These purple, gold, and red colors also were effective in grabbing the attention of those entering the neighborhood.

Start planting this recipe by placing the duranta in the center of the container. I always recommend wearing gloves when planting, but I especially recommend it when handling duranta, which can sometimes cause allergic reactions when folks come in contact with the sap from broken branches or crushed leaves. After planting the duranta, continue placing the remaining plants according to the recipe diagram.

This recipe is a good choice also for hard to reach column pots because so little maintenance is required. Water only when soil is dry to your touch or when you see a slight wilting of the duranta leaves. Feed monthly with a bloom-boosting fertilizer. 'Homestead Purple' verbena, during extreme heat, may rest from blooming until temperatures fall below the mid-90s. No pruning is needed for any of these plants throughout the growing season, but you may want to trim back the duranta in midsummer if you want a bushier look.

PLANT OPTIONS

Euonymus japonicus *'Aureo-marginatus'* could be substituted for Duranta *'Gold Edge'*. Purple petunias could be used if *'Homestead Purple'* verbenas are not available, although the petunias may need to be pruned back in midsummer.

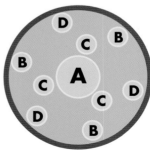

Spicy Ginger Pop

SUN PREFERENCE	CONTAINER SIZE	DIFFICULTY LEVEL
Partial Sun	Large	Easy

Shopping List

- Container mix potting soil
- 1 3-gallon-sized ginger (*Alpinia zerumbet*) **A**
- 3 summer snapdragons (*Angelonia* 'Angelface® Purple') **B**
- 3 verbenas (*Verbena* 'Aztec™ Dark Red') **C**
- 3 vinca vines (*Vinca minor* 'Illumination') **D**

Get ready for the party to begin once you've planted this colorful container recipe. This combination looks best in a dark colored container and is *extremely* vibrant in a cobalt blue planter. In milder climate zones, this recipe will do just fine in full sun, but the ginger and vinca vines need protection from the hot summer sun in warmer climates. The ginger also likes having room for its roots to grow and reach moisture so the deeper the container, the happier this plant will be.

Begin by filling your container a little over halfway with container mix potting soil, then loosen the soil around the rootball of the ginger. Center the ginger in the planter and add more soil around the rootball, bringing the soil level to within three inches of the top of the planter. When planting around a center plant in a container it is best to work your way out toward the rim of the planter, so plant the *Angelonia* next, followed by the verbenas, then finishing with the vincas. Add additional potting mix to fill in any spaces between the rootballs of the plants.

Maintaining this container recipe is very easy. When the leaves of the ginger begin to curl or roll instead of laying flat, it is telling you it needs a drink of water. Usually this occurs about the time that the top two inches of soil have dried out. Verbena has a tendency to bloom vigorously, then rest, then bloom, continuing this cycle throughout its growing season. While cutting off the faded blooms (deadheading) is not necessary for reblooming, some folks may prefer the cleaner look that occurs when it's deadheaded. Fertilize once a month during the growing season with a general-purpose plant food.

PLANT OPTIONS

Use Canna *'Tropicana' as a substitute for the ginger to give the containers a more vertical appeal. Red ivy geraniums make a good alternative to the red verbenas.*

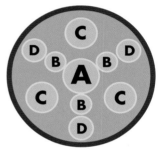

Spider Plant Flashback

SUN PREFERENCE	CONTAINER SIZE	DIFFICULTY LEVEL
Shade	Large	Easy

Shopping List

- Container mix potting soil
- 3 Persian shield (*Strobilanthes*) **A**
- 3 spider plants (*Chlorophytum comosum* 'Variegatum') **B**
- 6 impatiens (*Impatiens walleriana* 'Violet') **C**
- 3 creeping wire vines (*Muehlenbeckia axillaries*) **D**

Some of you reading this recipe may have fleeting memories from the 1960s and 1970s of macramé hanging baskets filled with a popular houseplant called spider plant. Fast forward to present day and you'll find the spider plant is a major component for many outdoor plantings, including this recipe's shade loving combination. It is hard to beat the textural interest that this plant provides amidst all the summer annual color.

A cool color mix of violet and white, with just a splash of purple, offers a welcome reprieve from summertime heat. After loosely filling your container with potting soil, place the spider plants at a slight angle toward the edge of the planter. Center the *Strobilanthes* in the middle of the container, then add the remaining plants according to the recipe diagram. The Persian shield may look a little small and out of proportion when first planted, but these plants grow extremely fast once they get established in the container and will make great center focal plants.

Care for this recipe is quite simple. Water only when the top of the soil is dry to your touch. The impatiens are the indicator plants to know when the soil has gotten a little too dry; if their leaves are wilting, it's time to water. Fertilize every other month with a general-purpose fertilizer.

In the fall, repot the spider plant and creeping wire vines into a container that you can bring indoors. Make sure that they have drainage while at the same time protecting your furniture or floors by placing a saucer under your planter to collect water. Or, plant these inside a plastic container that has drainage and place that container into a planter without drainage holes (a cachepot). Remove the inserted container to water in a sink or bathtub, allowing it to drain well and returning it to the outer container pot. Both of these plants are excellent indoor houseplants that like indirect light and need only weekly watering.

PLANT OPTIONS

Use Carex *'Frosted Curls' instead of the spider plant and enjoy the soft foliage of its blades (except then you can't call this recipe Spider Plant Flashback). If you want a more drought resistant but similar look, use a dark colored coleus instead of the Persian shield and pink angelwing begonias instead of the impatiens.*

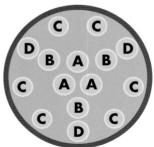

Spiky Color Burst

SUN PREFERENCE	CONTAINER SIZE	DIFFICULTY LEVEL
Full Sun	Extra Large	Intermediate

Shopping List

- Container mix potting soil
- 1 5-gallon-sized trellised mandevilla vine (*Mandevilla* 'Alice Du Pont') **A**
- 3 2-gallon-sized New Zealand flax (*Phormium* 'Sundowner') **B**
- 6 1-gallon-sized caladiums (*Caladium* 'Carolyn Whorton') **C**
- 3 2-gallon-sized spirea (*Spirea* x *bumalda* 'Goldflame') **D**
- 6 cupheas (*Cuphea llavea* 'Flamenco Samba') **E**
- 6 coleus (*Solenostemon* 'Trailing Cherry') **F**
- 3 black-eyed Susan vines (*Thunbergia alata*) **G**

One of the gals who has worked with me over the years is a master at putting together big, instant gratification container plantings. Yelena will look a gigantic planter in the eye and declare, "You don't intimidate me!" Then she works her creative magic to create recipes like this one. Combining small shrubs with tropical vines and colorful annuals, this sun-loving recipe had people circling the neighborhood to view it again.

In an extra-large planter, add enough container mix potting soil to fill the container at least halfway. Carefully remove the mandevilla vine from the pot it was grown in, keeping the vine attached to the trellis. Position the trellised vine in the middle of the planter and add enough soil to hold it in position but leaving room for the spireas and New Zealand flax. Once planted, these two-gallon plants will also help to hold the mandevilla in a vertical position. You *may* need to shave off a little around the diameter of the spireas and *Phormium* rootballs in order to place place them snugly together. Add the caladiums, followed by the cupheas, then the coleus and black-eyed Susan vines. Fill in any empty spaces between the rootballs of all these plants, leaving about one inch of space between the upper rim of the planter and the top of the soil.

For the first week or two, this planting will need to be watered daily. Once the roots have had a chance to get established, water only when the top two to three inches of soil are dry or when the black-eyed Susan vine looks a little wilted. Use a general-purpose fertilizer once a month to feed the plants in this container.

PLANT OPTIONS

In some climates either bougainvillea or passion vines may be easier to locate than mandevilla vines, and they are a great substitute for the trellised center plant. Use Vinca *'Cora Rose' or* Lantana *'Bandana Cherry' if cuphea is unavailable.*

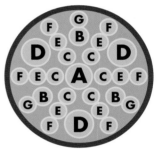

Strawberry and Licorice

SUN PREFERENCE	CONTAINER SIZE	DIFFICULTY LEVEL
Full Sun	Small	Easy

Shopping List

- Container mix potting soil
- 1 spike plant (*Dracaena*) **A**
- 1 licorice plant (*Helichrysum petiolare*) **B**
- 4 dark red ivy geraniums (*Pelargonium*) **C**
- 3 ivy geraniums (*Pelargonium* 'Blizzard Pink') **D**

This container recipe could also be called The Classic because it reminds me of the type of combinations that I first saw when I started container gardening: a spike plant, geraniums, and a licorice plant. This type of combination is often referred to as the *thriller* (spike plant), the *filler* (geraniums), and the *spiller* (licorice plant). The classic, simple look of these plants never goes out of style but the difference I see now is that the cultivars of these plants are so much more diverse and new-gardener friendly. A small container is all that you need to make this look, perfect for a table or atop a small column.

Pour enough container mix potting soil in your planter so that there is about three inches of space between the top of the soil and container rim. Place the spike plant as indicated by the recipe diagram. Arrange the geraniums in the container, leaving the licorice plant for last. Depending on the placement of your planter, the

licorice plant can be planted in the front of the container or it can appear to be spilling off to the side. Add any extra soil needed to cover all the roots of the plants, leaving about one inch of space from the top of the soil to the container rim.

Geraniums are big eaters, and they can use up the nutrients in the soil quickly, so you will want to fertilize this recipe once a month with a bloom-boosting fertilizer. Clean up the faded blooms, pinching off the stems down to the first set of leaves below the faded blossom. Water when the top two inches of soil are dry.

Licorice plant can grow quite long, especially in warmer climates. Rather than just trimming this back and throwing it all away, root it! Take a few cut branches and pull off 2 or 3 leaves closest to the cut edge and stick the cut end into a little vase of water to root. Once roots begin to grow, replant into another container.

PLANT OPTIONS

Plectranthus *can substitute for the licorice plant.* Cordyline *'Red Star' is an alternative to the spike plant for a more updated look in this recipe.*

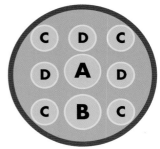

Subtle Exuberance

SUN PREFERENCE	CONTAINER SIZE	DIFFICULTY LEVEL
Partial Sun	Large	Easy

Shopping List

- Container mix potting soil
- 1 3-gallon-sized compact jatropha (*Jatropha integerrima* 'Compacta') **A**
- 1 1-gallon-sized variegated ginger (*Alpinia zerumbet* 'Variegata') **B**
- 1 Persian shield (*Strobilanthes dyerianus*) **C**
- 1 rose-scented geranium (*Pelargonium*) **D**
- 2 impatiens (*Impatiens walleriana*) **E**
- 3 chenille plants (*Acalypha hispida*) **F**

Another title for this container garden recipe could have been Grandma's House. Planted with soft, fuzzy chenille plants and rose-scented geraniums, a gentle brushing past this planting could send your thoughts over the hill and through the dale, to Grandmother's house we go. Use this recipe as a planting for your front door containers or for the planters near your favorite outdoor sitting area to benefit fully from the sensory pleasures of these different plants.

When putting this recipe together, the first plant in the container should be the *Jatropha*. Because several other plants need to be placed in this container in close proximity to the *Jatropha*, take the edge of a trowel or a hori-hori knife and shave off about 2 inches around the diameter of the rootball. After planting the *Jatropha*, add the variegated ginger, then finish planting with the remaining ingredients according to the recipe diagram.

This is not a fussy recipe that needs a lot of maintenance. Really, all that is needed is to take a little pinch off the top of the impatiens two or three times during the summer to encourage more branching on these plants. Also, the chenille plants are vigorous growers so you may need to trim them depending on the height of your container.

Fertilize once a month with a bloom-boosting plant food and water when the top of the soil is dry to touch. The rose-scented geranium can be put in a separate container in the fall and brought indoors during the colder weather to be enjoyed. Because it does not flower very often, it is an easy, low maintenance plant for a bright area by a window.

PLANT OPTIONS

You can try using a dark-leaved coleus such as 'Dark Star' or 'Merlot' as a substitute for the Strobilanthes *if you prefer.*

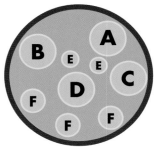

Summary Bold

SUN PREFERENCE	CONTAINER SIZE	DIFFICULTY LEVEL
Partial Sun	Medium	Easy

Shopping List

- Container mix potting soil
- 1 1-gallon-sized ivy geranium (*Pelargonium* 'Caliente Fire') **A**
- 2 purple queen (*Setcresea*) **B**
- 4 violas (*Viola* hybrid 'Penny Denim Jump-up') **C**
- 2 1-gallon-sized bougainvilleas (*Bougainvillea* 'Raspberry Ice') **D**
- 3 creeping wire vines (*Muehlenbeckia axillaries*) **E**

Window boxes are like earrings, an accessory that, once you've worn them, you don't ever want to be without. I planted these window boxes with this recipe when my client's home was still on the market. Once it sold, the new homeowners continued to keep this container planted. I think that the ease of care involved in this recipe encouraged the new owners to keep their window boxes planted with this recipe each season.

Ivy geraniums are fast growing once summer weather sets in so I don't usually suggest starting with anything larger than a 4-inch-sized plant. This recipe, however, uses the geranium as its focal plant so I recommend a 1-gallon-sized plant to give this recipe an instant impact in the window box. After centering the geranium in the container, plant the *Muehlenbeckia* in front of the geranium where it is spilling out over the edge of the window box. Plant the bougainvilleas next, tilting the plants slightly toward the *front* edge of the window box. This bougainvillea cultivar is used primarily for its foliage; the inconsequential purple blossoms that randomly occur should be considered pleasant surprises. Finally, finish planting the remaining plants according to recipe diagram. The violas may only be visible at first from inside the home, but they will eventually be seen peeking up behind the other plants.

Watering is needed only when the top of the soil is dry to the touch. Fertilize monthly with bloom-boosting plant food and pinch back the geranium flowers after the blooms have died.

PLANT OPTIONS

*I planted this window box in early spring and only
needed to substitute the violas with summer snapdragons
(Angelonia 'Serena Purple') to keep the look going through
the summer. Another variegated bougainvillea that I like
to use if 'Raspberry Ice' is not available is* Bougainvillea
'Golden Jackpot'.

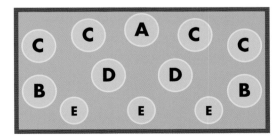

Summer Celebration

Shopping List

- Container mix potting soil
- 1 1-gallon-sized mandevilla (*Mandevilla* hybrid 'Sun Parasol Crimson') **A**
- 2 petunias (*Petunia* hybrid 'Royal Velvet') **B**
- 2 lantanas (*Lantana camara* 'Landmark Gold') **C**
- 2 verbenas (*Verbena* hybrid 'Aztec Dark Red') **D**
- 2 asparagus ferns (*Asparagus sprengeri*) **E**

Nonstop summer color greets you daily in this medium-sized container recipe. Easy to assemble, you'll want to place your one-gallon-sized mandevilla first in your soil-filled container, then plant the remaining plants according to the recipe diagram. These plant varieties all like to intertwine with one another without taking over the entire container.

Asparagus sprengeri, commonly called asparagus fern, adds an interesting texture to this planting with its needle looking leaves that contrast so well against the thick oval mandevilla leaves. The large, mounding flower heads of the verbenas are a nice companion to the rich, wide flowering heads of the petunias. Verbenas do have a tendency to bloom and rest throughout the summer so the mandevilla provides the consistent pop of red that makes this container recipe stand out.

With the full sun that Summer Celebration can handle, watering will need to be monitored during the hotter parts of the summer. This combination does not like to stay moist but a scorching summer day can dry out a medium-sized planter with this many plants pretty quickly. If you ever notice the potting mix start to shrink away from the edges of the planter, then it is time to give this container a good soaking. On the other hand, if you notice the leaves of the mandevilla start to yellow, then this planter is most likely getting too much water. If this happens, just lighten up on the watering and sprinkle a little Ironite® to green up the leaves.

With this much flowering going on, feeding your planting regularly is very important. Mark your summer calendar to fertilizer this planter once a month with a bloom-boosting plant food. Even though pruning is not needed to ensure reblooming, lantanas can benefit from pinching if you begin to see round green seeds develop. This is most often seen when the weather has been cool and wet or during the late summer season.

PLANT OPTIONS

Rather than using the red mandevilla in the center of this container,
substitute a red landscape or zonal geranium such as 'Patriot Red'. Or try
a one-gallon-sized Knock Out® rose if the container will be in a location so
that folks will not be brushing up against the thorns of the rose.

Summer Rain

SUN PREFERENCE	CONTAINER SIZE	DIFFICULTY LEVEL
Shade	Medium	Easy

Shopping List

- Container mix potting soil
- 3 umbrella grass plants (*Cyperus involucratus* 'Baby Tut') **A**
- 5 impatiens (*Impatiens walleriana* 'Butterfly Cherry') **B**
- 5 golden creeping jenny (*Lysimachia aurea*) **C**

If you have a shady spot and have a tendency to overwater, this may be a good option for you to try growing in your container. This recipe calls for only three different plant varieties but each variety is different enough in texture and color to provide a season-long interesting display.

Here's a little trick to keeping the moisture loving *Cyperus* happy in your container: Line the inside of the pots that the *Cyperus* came in with some type of plastic so that the holes do not allow drainage, then place the plant back in its pot. Plant the *Cyperus*, still in their pots, in the center of your container as shown by the recipe diagram. This will keep the roots of the *Cyperus* moist while allowing the other plants growing in the container to drain as needed. Make sure to plant deep enough in your container that the *Cyperus* inner pots are not showing above the soil line.

Impatiens can always benefit from pinching two or three inches off the top of the plant at midsummer to encourage the plant to grow fuller and bushier. Often this will involve pinching off blooming plants or buds, which is always hard to do, but the benefit will be seen within just a few weeks with an increased display of color.

Water when top of the soil around the impatiens and golden creeping jenny is dry. Ideally, the soil around the *Cyperus* will stay moist throughout the summer. Fertilize at midsummer with a general-purpose plant food.

Creeping jenny is hardy to zone 2 so don't discard it with your other annuals. Reuse it in your fall and winter containers in zones 5 and warmer. It is considered invasive in certain areas so check with your local Extension agent before replanting in the landscape.

PLANT OPTIONS

The options that would give this same effect would be to use a cultivar of Torenia fournieri *like 'Golden Moon' or 'Clown Rose' instead of impatiens, and* Lysimachia *'Persian Chocolate' instead of* Lysimachia aurea.

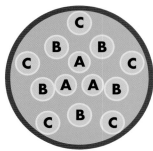

Summer Sparkler

SUN PREFERENCE	CONTAINER SIZE	DIFFICULTY LEVEL
Full Sun	Large	Easy

Shopping List

- Container mix potting soil
- 1 3-gallon-sized variegated flax lily (*Dianella tasmanica* 'Variegata') **A**
- 5 ivy geraniums (*Pelargonium* 'Freestyle® Ruby Red') **B**
- 5 euphorbias (*Euphorbia graminea* 'Diamond Frost®') **C**
- 3 verbenas (*Verbena* 'Lanai® Blue') **D**

Like a Fourth of July sparkler, this combo is an *explosion* of textures that will brighten an area, especially when placed in front of evergreens or a dark background. This sun-loving combo needs little deadheading, blooms best when kept on the dry side, and will keep going from spring until frost. What more do you want?

The accent piece of this recipe is the *Dianella*, which blooms throughout the summer with delicate, light blue flowers that dance over your arrangement during a gentle breeze. Trailing down the sides of your container will be the dark blue verbenas, whose thick clusters of flowers bring a bold color border. Filling in between the verbenas and the *Dianella* are explosive bursts of white *Euphorbia* 'Diamond Frost' and blasts of red from the geraniums. If you substitute the *Euphorbia* with *Gypsophilia paniculata* 'Baby's Breath' or *Lobularia maritima* 'Snow Princess™', the 'Snow Princess' will drape more heavily than the *Euphorbia* so you will lose some of that "sparkler" effect.

Flowering annuals are heavy feeders so fertilize monthly throughout the growing season with a product that encourages flower blooming. While pinching off old blooms is not necessary to keep your geraniums flowering, it does help give your planting a clean look. You'll love the way the strong, thin stems of euphorbias wind their way through the other plants, echoing the white edge of the *Dianella*. Good foliage contrasts between the big round leaves of the geranium, the tall thick blades of flax lily, the dainty oval euphorbia leaves, and the finely serrated verbena give this combo interest way beyond its patriotic color palette.

PLANT OPTIONS

If you have a hard time locating flax lily, look for either Cordyline australis *'Alberti' or ribbon grass* Phalaris arundinacea *'Strawberries & Cream' as a similar substitute with green-and-white foliage. You won't get the delicate blue flowers with these other plants but they will maintain the vertical impact. The geraniums can be substituted with* Petunia *'Easy Wave Red' or* Cuphea llavea *'Totally Tempted' to maintain that pop of red. You could easily substitute the verbenas with* Calibrachoa *Superbells® 'Trailing Blue' or* Scaevola *'New Wonder®'.*

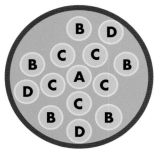

Sweet Dreams

SUN PREFERENCE	CONTAINER SIZE	DIFFICULTY LEVEL
Full Sun	Medium	Easy

Shopping List

- Container mix potting soil
- 1 1-gallon-sized pink flowering maple (*Abutilon* x *hybridum* 'Roseus') **A**
- 3 dwarf dahlias (*Dahlia* 'Goldalia™ Rose') **B**
- 5 summer snapdragons (*Angelonia* 'Angelface Pink') **C**
- 3 fan flowers (*Scaevola* 'Bombay Pink') **D**
- 3 fan flowers (*Scaevola* 'Bombay Blue') **E**

The first time I saw a flowering maple with its delicate, upside-down flowers I thought, "I have got to find a place to showcase this plant!" But I wanted folks to see the flowers from underneath, and I don't know very many people who will get down on their hands and knees to look up at a flower. Then I thought about all the containers that I locate on columns and realized that I had found a showcase spot for the *Abutilon*.

When you start putting this recipe together, place the *Abutilon* in the center of the container. Don't worry about planting the remaining plants too close to the *Abutilon* because this little tropical shrub has an open, airy form that allows other plants to get enough light and to grow through the lower branches. This recipe is a good choice for containers that are difficult to reach because little pruning is needed. The dahlias will keep a cleaner look if you maintain a little pinching back of flowers that have finished blooming.

Watering requirements involve watering only when the top of the soil is dry to the touch. All the plants in this recipe are heavy bloomers so I recommend feeding once a month with bloom-boosting fertilizer.

This recipe is most striking when planted in a black or dark gray planter. Or eliminate the blue fan flower—substitute three additional pink fan flowers—and use a brown planter. The effect is very current and in vogue.

PLANT OPTIONS

*Different cultivars of each plant variety are available
for substituting if the specific cultivar mentioned in
this recipe is not available.*

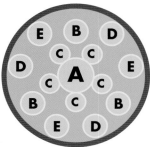

Tabletop Beauty

SUN PREFERENCE	CONTAINER SIZE	DIFFICULTY LEVEL
Partial Sun	Small	Easy

Shopping List

- Container mix potting soil
- 1 1-gallon-sized hibiscus (*Hibiscus rosa-sinensis* 'Red Wave') **A**
- 2 verbenas (*Verbena* hybrid 'Babylon Red') **B**
- 1 golden creeping jenny (*Lysimachia aurea*) **C**
- 1 sweet flag grass (*Acorus gramineus* 'Ogon') **D**

My patio is my favorite room in my house, which is somewhat of a paradox since it is not actually *in* my house. But whether I'm sitting out there with my morning cup of tea watching the colors of the sunrise or sharing supper with my family, I love how a small pot of flowers can make every occasion feel special. This recipe provides a season-long beauty wherever you are inspired to place it.

If you plan to place this small container on an outdoor dinner table, choose a container that is no more than six inches high. With any planter higher than that you might have to remove it from the table to be able to see your guests. When putting the recipe together, shave about an inch diameter off the rootball using the edge of a trowel or a hori-hori knife, then plant it as shown in the recipe diagram. The remaining plants will need to have a little of the soil loosened around

their roots for everything to fit snugly in the container. This is done with your fingers gently massaging the rootballs, allowing some soil to drop off and making the roots pliable enough to squeeze easily into the planter. Add the *Acorus* and *Lysimachia* next, then finish with the verbenas.

This is a quick and easy container to put together, but a smaller container can require a little more watering upkeep because there is less soil to retain moisture. A container this size usually can be watered every day except during rainy or cooler days. If the top of the soil feels dry to your touch, give this planter a drink of water. Also, fertilize once a month with a bloom-boosting plant food. Several times throughout the season you may want to pinch back the verbenas and *Lysimachia* as it starts to spread out over your table. Or you could let it keep growing as an all-natural tablecloth!

PLANT OPTIONS

If you want the darker foliage of the hibiscus, but don't want the frequent falling blossoms of the flowers, substitute ornamental peppers such as Capsicum *'Black Pearl' or 'Purple Flash'.*

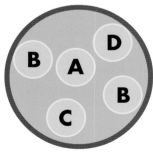

Tropical Flower Child

SUN PREFERENCE	CONTAINER SIZE	DIFFICULTY LEVEL
Full Sun	Large	Easy

Shopping List

- Container mix potting soil
- 1 3-gallon-sized tropical hibiscus (*Hibiscus rosa-sinensis* 'Double Pink') **A**
- 3 licorice plants (*Helichrysum petiolare*) **B**
- 3 verbenas (*Verbena* 'Homestead Purple') **C**
- 6 ivy geraniums (*Pelargonium* 'Caliente® Rose') **D**

Few plants can compare in flower power to the tropical hibiscus. Its large blossoms are great for grabbing attention across the lawn or standing out even in the midst of other bold colors. When you want to draw attention to your front door or a special spot in your garden, use this simple recipe as a quick and easy "look at me!" solution.

The first thing you will want to do after filling your planter about three-fourths full of container mix potting soil is to loosen soil around the roots of the hibiscus bush. If the roots are very dense, use the edge of your trowel to make one-half-inch slices down the sides of the rootball to encourage the roots to spread out into the surrounding soil. After placing the hibiscus in position, pour additional potting mix around the roots to bring the soil level up for the remaining plants. Add the geraniums, then plant the verbenas and licorice plants with a slight tilt toward the *outside* of the planter. Make sure that the roots are covered with potting mix but still have about an inch of space below the rim of the planter.

With this many heavily flowering plants, you may want to fertilize once a week with a bloom-booster fertilizer that has been diluted to half strength. Water when the top two inches of soil are dry to touch, or watch the leaves of the hibiscus; when it first starts to droop, that's your indication that it is time to water. If the hibiscus leaves start to yellow, check to make sure that you are not giving too much water and fertilize with a plant food that includes iron. Remove any fallen hibiscus blossoms that may have dropped on the plants below so that they don't smother any foliage or flowers. This recipe is happiest when it's in sun, but for those in hotter climates you will find that this recipe performs just as well in part sun.

PLANT OPTIONS

Use Lantana *'Luscious™ Grape' as a substitute for the verbena and* Evolvulus *'Blue Daze' instead of the licorice plant if you want even more flowers.*

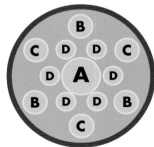

Tropical Paradise

SUN PREFERENCE	CONTAINER SIZE	DIFFICULTY LEVEL
Shade	Extra Large	Moderate

Shopping List

- Container mix potting soil
- 1 5-gallon-sized tropical palm (*Chamaerops humilis* 'European Fan Palm') **A**
- 3 1-gallon-sized caladiums (*Caladium* 'White Queen') **B**
- 6 wishbone flowers (*Torenia* 'Summer Wave Blue') **C**
- 2 1-gallon-sized begonias (*Begonia* 'Black Velvet') **D**

When I first started working with my co-worker Yelena, this recipe was one of the first she put together where I saw her wonderful eye for design. Hopefully, this container recipe will be repeated often and folks across the country can enjoy it as much as I do!

As with any extra-large container planting, place your container where you plan on keeping it *before* you start adding soil and putting the recipe together. I've found that I often have to cut the plastic container off the rootballs of palms because the roots may be tightly contained within the pot, so keep some hand-pruners close by. Keep the rootball intact and do not try to loosen the soil around the rootball as I have recommended for many other larger-sized plants. The palm will need to be planted first because of its size and because the remaining ingredients are positioned around it. The palm's rootball will take up a lot of room in the container so only fill the planter halfway with container mix potting soil before placing the palm as indicated in the recipe diagram. Loosely add more potting soil around the rootball, leaving about four inches from the top of the container, and plant the caladiums, then the begonias. If needed, add a little more potting soil before finishing with the *Torenia*. Be careful not to bury the trunk of the palm with potting soil or it will develop trunk rot.

Very little maintenance is needed with this recipe. Keep this planting slightly on the dry side by only watering when the top two inches of soil feel dry. The *Torenia* is a nice indicator plant for when watering is needed; when it starts looking droopy, it's time to water, because it is the first plant to suffer from lack of water. Fertilize in midsummer with a general-purpose fertilizer. Regularly trim off faded or browning palm fronds.

A word to the wise: wear thick gardening gloves when handling the palm, which can have some sharp spines along its trunk as it matures.

PLANT OPTIONS

Windmill palm,
Trachycarpus fortunei,
is a good substitute for the
European fan palm, with
the added benefit of being
cold hardy to zone 6.
Lobelia siphilitica *can be*
used instead of the Torenia,
especially in areas where
summer temperatures rarely
get out of the mid-80s.

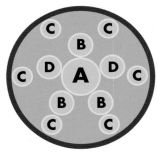

A Twist Of Lime

SUN PREFERENCE	CONTAINER SIZE	DIFFICULTY LEVEL
Full Sun	Medium	Easy

Shopping List

- Container mix potting soil
- 1 1-gallon-sized lantana (*Lantana* hybrid 'Tropical Temptation Mimosa') **A**
- 2 coleus (*Solenostemon* 'Golda') **B**
- 1 1-gallon-sized mandevilla (*Mandevilla* hybrid 'Sun Parasol® Crimson') **C**
- 2 sedums (*Sedum repestre* 'Angelina') **D**

The word "refreshing" comes to mind when I look at this container. Bright and cheery, this low maintenance, sun-loving combination sends out a welcome call to all who pass by.

Fill your planters with container mix potting soil, leaving about four inches between the soil and the rim of the planter. Add the lantana and the mandevilla, but make sure that you have taken the time to loosen their rootballs before planting. Next, add the coleus, slightly tilting the plants toward the outer rim of the planter. Last, place the sedums so that they are spilling over the edge of the container.

The new bush-type mandevillas are a hybrid of a mandevilla and dipledenia; they are excellent bloomers during the heat of the summer. They do, however, send out random long vines that can either be left to add an artistic flair to this recipe

or trimmed back to keep a more uniform look to this planting. Pinch off any of the green, round seed clusters that may form on the lantana so that the plant is using its energy toward blooming rather than seed making. If the coleus begins to look a little scraggly, pinch off the top two inches right above a set of leaves.

Water when the top two inches of soil are dry to the touch. You can also use the coleus as an indicator for watering because its leaves will droop when the planting is thirsty. Fertilize once a month with a general-purpose fertilizer.

Here's a little recycling tip for your container planting: the sedum variety used in this recipe is hardy to zone 3 and has a nice rosy-bronze tone to it during the winter months. Reuse this plant in your winter plantings or plant in the ground as a beautiful, drought-tolerant groundcover.

PLANT OPTIONS

Alternathera *'Chartreuse'* is an easy substitute for the coleus. It may be easier to locate Lantana *'Athens Rose'* than *'Tropical Temptation Mimosa'*.

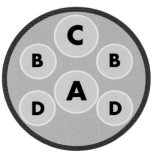

Wishing Well

SUN PREFERENCE	CONTAINER SIZE	DIFFICULTY LEVEL
Shade	Large	Moderate

Shopping List

- Container mix potting soil
- 1 3-gallon-sized elephant ears (*Colocasia esculenta* 'Black Magic') **A**
- 3 1-gallon-sized variegated sweet flag (*Acorus calamus* 'Variegatus') **B**
- 3 tall umbrella plants (*Cyperus alternifolius*) **C**
- 5 golden creeping jenny (*Lysimachia aurea*) **D**

I spotted this luscious container recipe on a tour I took of Montrose Gardens in Hillsborough, North Carolina. I've replicated this design several times in containers where the drainage holes have a tendency to get plugged up and hold water because all of the plants in this recipe are moisture loving.

Begin by planting the 3-gallon-sized *Colocasia* in the container according the diagram placement. Don't be too concerned if several of the long-stemmed leaves are broken in the planting process; after you have finished planting everything in the container, cut the damaged stems off at the base of the plant. They will be replaced quickly with new growth. Continue planting with the variegated sweet flag grass. Next, plant the *Cyperus alternifolius*, but you may notice that these plants look disproportionately small compared to the other plants. They will grow extremely fast and form the backdrop to this delightful combination of black-and-white and contrasting forms. Finally, plant the creeping jenny, and water it all in. This is one of the few times that you will ever hear me say, "Don't worry about watering too much." The main rule to follow here is to never let the soil dry out. Fertilize in midsummer with a general-purpose fertilizer.

I have placed this recipe in a shade category, but in milder climates these plants can grow well in part sun.

In mild climates, you can maintain this recipe in a container year-round. Most of the plants will die back or look a little ratty during the winter, but cut back all the foliage in early spring for fresh new growth.

PLANT OPTIONS

Because they have similar moist soil requirements, the Japanese iris variety Iris kaempferi variegata *is easily interchangeable with the* Acorus calamus *'Variegatus'. With the iris you will also get its short-lived but regal blue blooms.*

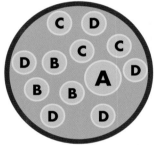

A U T U M N

Bamboozled

SUN PREFERENCE	CONTAINER SIZE	DIFFICULTY LEVEL
Partial Sun	Extra Large	Easy

Shopping List

- Container mix potting soil
- 3 1-gallon-sized bamboo plants (*Fargesia rufa* 'Sunset Glow') **A**
- 2 1-gallon-sized variegated gold dust plants (*Acuba japonica* 'Variegata') **B**
- 1 1-gallon-sized bush honeysuckle (*Lonicera nitida* 'Edmee Gold') **C**
- 2 1-gallon-sized sweet flag grass (*Acorus gramineus* 'Ogon') **D**
- 2 1-gallon-sized coral bells (*Heuchera* 'Montrose Ruby') **E**

I once heard a plantsman tell a group that, "friends don't let friends plant bamboo." Having grown up in the middle of Georgia, where bamboo was taking over my neighborhood, I could understand where he was coming from! But that was before I learned about *Fargesia rufa*, and before I realized how *delightful* bamboo is in a container planting. This is a clumping, slow-growing, short evergreen bamboo that adds texture and movement to any container recipe.

Since this recipe has a distinct front and back to the design, the easiest way to plant is to begin with the plants in the back and work forward. Start by planting the bamboo, then place the *Acuba* as indicated by the recipe design. Next,

when planting the sweet flag grass, tilt the plants toward the sides of the planter, away from the bamboo and gold dust plants. Finally, when planting the honeysuckle and coral bells slightly tilt these toward the front of the planter. Even in this extra-large planter this many one-gallon-sized plants may be a little squished. If needed, shave off about one-half inch around the diameter of the bamboo and *Acuba* rootballs.

Keep this planting evenly moist by watering only when the top of the soil feels dry to your touch. Gardeners in zones 6 and warmer can use this recipe as a winter or year-round planting, in which case you will need to fertilize in the early spring and midsummer with a general-purpose plant food.

PLANT OPTIONS

A more dramatic look can be created by using the taller black bamboo Phyllostachys nigra.

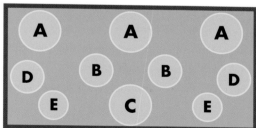

The Big Three

SUN PREFERENCE	CONTAINER SIZE	DIFFICULTY LEVEL
Full Sun	Large	Easy

Shopping List

- Container mix potting soil
- 1 5-gallon-sized dwarf golden arborvitae (*Thuja orientalis* 'Aurea nana') **A**
- 4 kale (*Brassica oleracea* 'Red Bor') **B**
- 8 yellow pansies (*Viola* x *wittrockiana*) **C**
- 4 red pansies (*Viola* x *wittrockiana*) **D**

Every year since I have been planting containers professionally, there are a few plants that remain my staple ingredients for fall and winter plantings. This recipe combines the faithful three plants that I can count on to never give me any trouble and still make a statement of color and beauty. Also, one of the nice aspects of this recipe is that all of these plants are relatively inexpensive. It looks good, it loves full sun, it's easy care, and it's inexpensive—so you're probably wondering, "What's the catch?" Well, this is one of those fall plantings that is truly just a fall planting for my friends in zones colder than zone 6. Many of my other fall recipes can either be overwintered with few or no substitutions, but this one would require a whole new recipe to carry over through the spring for those in colder climates. That being said, the *Thuja* is an easy shrub to overwinter indoors in a heated, windowed garage or a sunny, heated porch.

To put this recipe together, begin by taking the edge of a trowel or a hori-hori knife (a super great Japanese style knife with a serrated edge) and trim around the diameter of the *Thuja* rootball. This allows you to snuggle the remaining plants up a little closer to the *Thuja*, providing an instant gratification look to the container. Fill the planter about two-thirds of the way with container mix potting soil. Plant according to the recipe diagram, placing the arborvitae first before adding more soil and the remaining ingredients. When planting the kale, tilt the plant slightly away from the arborvitae so that it is not growing directly into the branches.

Water when the top 2 to 3 inches of soil are dry. Fertilize the pansies monthly with a bloom-boosting plant food.

PLANT OPTIONS

It should not be difficult to find all of these plants but just remember it's a fall-only container recipe for some areas.

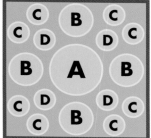

Bright Camellias

SUN PREFERENCE	CONTAINER SIZE	DIFFICULTY LEVEL
Shade	Large	Easy

Shopping List

- Container mix potting soil
- 1 5-gallon-sized camellia (*Camellia japonica* 'Winter's Fancy') **A**
- 2 1-gallon-sized bush honeysuckles (*Lonicera* 'Edmee Gold') **B**
- 3 1-gallon-sized coral bells (*Heuchera* 'Caramel') **C**
- 5 vincas (*Vinca minor* 'Illumination') **D**

There are few plants that bring back as many pleasant memories as camellias provide for me. Where I grew up in Georgia, camellia blossoms were a part of the Thanksgiving dinner decorations, floating in a bowl of water surrounded by the bowl of black-eyed peas and squash casserole. I *love* to use camellias in container recipes because their glossy oval leaves and plethora of blossoms are hard to find in very many other plants during the cooler seasons. For those in areas colder than zone 6, this is one plant worth wintering over indoors to enjoy during your milder seasons.

These four evergreen plants, for those in zone 6 and warmer, allow for some bright color in your shady areas. Even when 'Winter's Fancy' camellia is not blooming, the 'Edmee Gold' honeysuckle is lighting up the container with its chartreuse color. In warmer climates, choose more cold hardy camellias if you can't find this cultivar because the cold hardy ones tend to do better in containers. Also remember that, depending on the variety, camellias can bloom anytime from early fall to spring so make sure you have a fall-blooming camellia to make the most of this autumn recipe.

Place the camellia first in your planter to establish proper spacing, then plant the 'Edmee Gold' honeysuckle slightly angled toward the outer rim of the planter. Next, nestle the 'Caramel' coral bells between the honeysuckle and behind the camellia, and fill in any gaps between the root systems of the plants with extra soil. Finally, fill in the areas as shown by the plant recipe with 'Illumination' vinca. Don't allow this planting to dry out and keep soil evenly moist but not saturated with water. Camellias bloom best when grown in acidic soil. Before placing camellias in the planter, put a teaspoon of used coffee grinds or a teaspoon of Espoma Hollytone® under each camellia rootball.

PLANT OPTIONS

Several other cultivars of camellia that could be substituted are 'Winter's Fire', 'Autumn Rose', and 'Winter's Star'. Other cultivars of Heuchera could be used, such as 'Southern Comfort' or 'Amber Waves'.

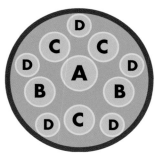

Coral Bark Queen

SUN PREFERENCE	CONTAINER SIZE	DIFFICULTY LEVEL
Partial Sun	Large	Easy

Shopping List

- Container mix potting soil
- 1 5-gallon-sized coral bark maple (*Acer palmatum* 'Sango-kaku') **A**
- 3 1-gallon-sized boxwoods (*Buxus* 'Glencoe') **B**
- 3 purple-leafed wintercreepers (*Euonymus fortunei* 'Coloratus') **C**
- 6 yellow pansies (*Viola* x *wittrockiana*) **D**

When planting fall and winter planters, you *may* need to adjust your perspective of horticultural beauty. Looking beyond the well-loved flowering plants of spring and summer, beauty can be found in the contrast of textures, in the elegant forms of defoliated trees and shrubs, and in the transition of foliage color that autumn is famous for when you live in temperate zones.

One of the most striking plants to watch during the fall is the coral bark maple. As temperatures begin to cool, the lime green leaves of the coral bark maple become golden and its red bark color begins to intensify. When paired with the purple-leafed wintercreeper, whose foliage also transitions from deep green to burgundy-purple with the cooling temperatures, this recipe begs to be noticed wherever it is positioned. The yellow pansies first mirror the coral bark maple's leaves, and then serve as a brilliant contrast to its bright red bark. The boxwoods are the classic "skirt" that carries this stately beauty through its transitions.

As you plan on putting this recipe together, start early enough to be able to watch the transition of color on the coral bark maple. Once you've gathered all your material, plant the coral bark maple first to center it; secure it with soil around the rootball so it is not leaning. Next, plant the boxwoods closely around the base of the coral bark maple. Finally, plant the pansies and wintercreepers as shown in the recipe diagrams.

Water when the top of the soil is dry to the touch and fertilize the pansies each month with a bloom-boosting fertilizer.

PLANT OPTIONS

Substituting a red twig dogwood, Cornus alba *'Sibirica', for the coral bark maple is an option for folks in areas colder than zone 5. The red bark is similar, but the artistic form of the coral bark maple will be missing with this substitution.*

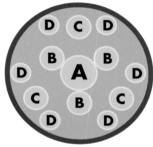

Dandy Deckbox

SUN PREFERENCE	CONTAINER SIZE	DIFFICULTY LEVEL
Shade	Medium	Easy

Shopping List

- Container mix potting soil
- 1 1-gallon-sized bergenia (*Bergenia cordifolia* 'Winterglut') **A**
- 2 1-gallon-sized coral bells (*Heuchera* 'Palace Purple') **B**
- 2 1-gallon-sized camellias (*Camellia japonica* 'Spring's Promise') **C**

If you've never met bergenia, let me help you get acquainted. You've already seen *Heuchera* and camellias used throughout this container recipe book because they work well either as an accent plant or as the focal plant in a container, and because they faithfully perform well in container plantings. Then along comes bergenia with its dramatic foliage. Bergenia reminds me a little of my oldest brother who walks into a gathering and, just with his big, fun personality alone, can grab the entire room's attention. When bergenia is used in a container planting, it may take you a moment to notice the other plants. *Bergenia* 'Winterglut' also can survive in a wide range of climates ranging from zone 3 to zone 9. As the temperatures cool off in the fall, bergenia foliage takes on shades of pink, purple, and burgundy.

Locate a shady spot where you plan on placing your container. When planting window boxes or any rectangular planter, it is easier to start planting with the plants that are farthest away from where you are positioned. For example, if you are leaning out a window to plant this recipe in a window box, plant the coral bells in the corners first, then add the bergenia, and finish planting with the camellias. When using all the one-gallon-sized plants that are listed in this recipe, only fill the container halfway with the potting soil. After positioning all the plants in the container, add any extra potting soil that is needed to fill in the spaces between the plants.

Water this planting when the top of the soil is dry to your touch. In zones 6 through zone 9, this recipe can be used as a year-round planting. The folks in those zones who want to maintain these throughout the year will want to fertilize in the early spring and late summer with a general-purpose fertilizer.

PLANT OPTIONS

To carry this planting through the winter in climates colder than zone 6, substitute a red twig dogwood, Cornus alba, *for the camellias.*

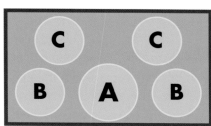

Fall's Folly

SUN PREFERENCE	CONTAINER SIZE	DIFFICULTY LEVEL
Sun	Large	Easy

Shopping List

- Container mix potting soil
- 1 3-gallon-sized fernspray false cypress (*Chamaecyparis obtusa* 'Filicoides') **A**
- 2 1-gallon-sized false hollies (*Osmanthus heterophyllus* 'Goshiki') **B**
- 2 1-gallon-sized Swiss chard (*Beta vulgaris* 'Bright Lights') **C**
- 1 1-gallon-sized kale (*Brassica oleracea* 'Red Bor') **D**
- 6 yellow pansies (*Viola* x *wittrockiana*) **E**

Mixing edibles and ornamental plants in the landscape has been a design tool for many years. It allows efficient use of available land, while permitting an appealing landscape display throughout the year. This same design idea can be applied to containers on a smaller scale as shown by this container recipe. The ever-popular fernspray false cypress provides an interesting display of evergreen foliage to work around, and the *Osmanthus* 'Goshiki' provides a great backdrop for the colorful Swiss chard. What fun to snip off a few leaves of the Swiss chard and kale to brighten an autumn salad, and then accent with a few candied pansy flowers!

I use a large rectangular planter for this container recipe and recommend placing the planter where you would want it before adding soil. Once planted, even with these newer fiberglass planters, the containers are extremely heavy to relocate. Fill the planter about halfway with container mix potting soil and center the fernspray false cypress as indicated in the plant diagram. Make sure that the top of the rootball on the fernspray is only about one inch below the rim of the planter. You want the limbs to be high enough to accommodate the remaining plants. At this point you may want to add some more soil but you should still leave room for adding the one-gallon-sized plants. When planting the false hollies, angle them slightly away from the fernspray false cypress. Next, as you plant the 'Red Bor' kale, angle away from the fernspray also, allowing some of the leaves to spill over the edge of the planter. Finally, plant the Swiss chard and the pansies as shown on the diagram.

This easy care container recipe needs only to be watered when the top two inches of soil has dried. Fertilize once a month with a general-purpose fertilizer. If you are growing the kale and Swiss chard for ornamental purposes only, pinch off any older leaves throughout the season to maintain a cleaner look in your container.

PLANT OPTIONS

In climates warmer than zone 8, camellias or Gardenia
jasminoides *'August Beauty' would be fun to substitute for the
fernspray false cypress, giving the added benefit of delightful
fragrance and flowers.* Gaultheria procumbens, *commonly
called creeping wintergreen, could be used for the false holly in
climates colder than zone 6.*

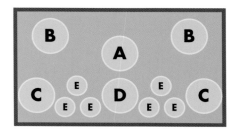

Fall Window Dressing

SUN PREFERENCE	CONTAINER SIZE	DIFFICULTY LEVEL
Full Sun	Large	Easy

Shopping List

- Container mix potting soil
- 1 1-gallon-sized kale (*Brassica oleracea* 'Red Bor') **A**
- 2 1-gallon-sized coral bells (*Heuchera* 'Caramel') **B**
- 4 purple wintercreepers (*Euonymus fortunei* 'Coloratus') **C**
- 2 1-gallon-sized Swiss chard (*Beta vulgaris* 'Bright Lights') **D**
- Assortment of cut branches from 6 inches to 2 ½ feet (approximately 10 to 12, of evergreen magnolia branches, lichen covered dead branches, pyracantha berries, or other winter berry branches from plants such as yaupon hollies or nandinas). **E**

This container recipe will allow us to "branch out"—please pardon the pun—from the other recipes because it doesn't involve using growing plants exclusively. This recipe, a favorite of one of the gals who works with me, is in fact different every time we put one together because its look depends on the type of branches that can be located at planting time. There are a few plants that will be planted in the soil of this window box, but the best effect is achieved by the placement of the various branches. As fall slips away into winter, these branches will be replaced by brightly colored balls and red ribbon for the holidays.

Fill your window box or rectangular container three-fourths with container mix potting soil. As seen in the planting diagram, plant the one-gallon-sized plants along the front or outward-facing side of the window box. Fill in extra soil if needed before planting the smaller plants.

All of these plants in this recipe are low maintenance plants that like the soil to be slightly on the dry side. That being said, hayrack window boxes do tend to dry out faster than other containers, so check the soil often throughout the week and water when the top two inches of soil are dry. Fertilize once a month with a general-purpose fertilizer.

After you have planted the growing plants, stick the branches that you have gathered randomly behind the planted material, placing at an angle and using at least 3 different varieties. The moisture in the soil will help keep the branches looking fresh, and every once in a while you might even get a branch to take root! Depending on the location of this container and of your house, you may need to replenish the branches with berries if the birds decide to snack on them.

PLANT OPTIONS

Heuchera *options include substituting other cultivars like 'Southern Comfort' or, for more red tones, 'Fire Chief'. Vinca 'Illumination' would be a colorful substitute for the wintercreeper.*

Fiery Crotons

SUN PREFERENCE	CONTAINER SIZE	DIFFICULTY LEVEL
Partial Sun	Large	Easy

Shopping List

- Container mix potting soil
- 3 1-gallon-sized coral bells (*Heuchera* 'Caroline') **A**
- 1 1-gallon-sized croton (*Codiaeum* 'Petra') **B**
- 2 1-gallon-sized crotons (*Codiaeum* 'Batik') **C**
- 1 1-gallon-sized Japanese blood grass (*Imperata cylindrica* 'Red Baron') **D**

Crotons have long been a staple of the indoor plant palette. Their coloring, however, is *perfect* for blending with the shades of autumn both in nature and in fall décor. In this recipe I've used 'Petra' and 'Batik,' but you'll enjoy looking through your local garden centers at all the cultivars of croton; you may find options that you like better than these two. The Japanese blood grass provides a good textural contrast to the heavy leaves of the croton.

At first glance, the *Heuchera* that I have chosen here may seem an odd choice, but as the temperatures cool off the foliage of *Heuchera* 'Caroline' deepen to a purple-bronze that frames the orange and red fiery colors above it. When I first planted this cultivar of *Heuchera*, it reminded me of the white-hot coals under an autumn campfire. Position the three crotons first by following the recipe diagram when you start putting this planting together. The Japanese blood grass, depending on how long the plant has been in its one-gallon-sized pot, may look a little out of proportion when positioned in its spot in the container, but the grass will quickly fill in and up to balance the design. When planting the coral bells, slightly tilt the plants toward the outside edge to give the effect of them spilling over the sides.

Keep the soil slightly on the dry side by waiting to water until the top two inches of soil are dry to your touch. Fertilize every three months with a general-purpose fertilizer if you plan on keeping this recipe in the container for more than one season, or if you plan on using this as a recipe during the colder months as an indoor plant. (Yes, it can be moved indoors.)

PLANT OPTIONS

You should be able to find all the plants in this recipe no matter where your zone is.

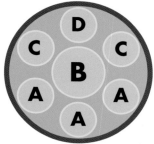

Glorious Greens

SUN PREFERENCE	CONTAINER SIZE	DIFFICULTY LEVEL
Shade	Large	Easy

Shopping List

- Container mix potting soil
- 1 3-gallon-sized variegated gold dust plant (*Acuba japonica* 'Variegata') **A**
- 2 1-gallon-sized camellias (*Camellia* hybrid 'Winter's Star') **B**
- 1 1-gallon-sized bush honeysuckle (*Lonicera nitida* 'Edmee Gold') **C**
- 2 6-inch-sized English ivies (*Hedera helix*) **D**
- 2 stonecrops (*Sedum reflexum* 'Angelina') **E**

This is one of those container recipes that I rely on often for that deep shade spot that is hard to find plants for. All of the plants in this recipe can tolerate that full shade condition, including the *Sedum* 'Angelina'. The *Lonicera* 'Edmee Gold' seems to glow in the shade and its coloring brings out the gold flecks in the 'Variegata' gold dust plant.

Whenever you are putting together a container recipe, most often you should start assembling the combination by planting the largest plant first. After loosening the soil around the rootball of the gold dust plant, place it in the container that has been partially filled with container mix potting soil. Add more soil after the *Acuba* is planted so that the plants are not sitting too low in the container. Next, the camellias will need to be planted,

followed by the bush honeysuckle. Finish planting the remaining plants according to the recipe diagram. You may need to add additional soil to fill in gaps around the plants.

Keep this planting evenly moist by watering only when the top of the soil feels dry to your touch. Gardeners in zones 6 and warmer can use this recipe as a winter or year-round planting, in which case you will need to fertilize in the early spring and midsummer with a general-purpose plant food. I have noticed that *Acuba* leaves will droop significantly when temperatures are below freezing. While unsightly, they will perk back up when the temperatures rise above freezing. Bring this container indoors during the winter if you live in zones 5 and colder. Keep it in indirect light and water once a week.

PLANT OPTIONS

This is another recipe that should be available, plant-wise, in all parts of the country. You could use a green-and-gold colored Croton *as a substitute for the* Acuba.

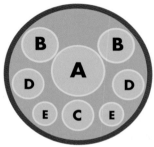

A Happy Little Planting

SUN PREFERENCE	CONTAINER SIZE	DIFFICULTY LEVEL
Partial Sun	Medium	Easy

Shopping List

- Container mix potting soil
- 1 1-gallon-sized sweet flag grass (*Acorus gramineus* 'Ogon') **A**
- 1 blackbird spurge (*Euphorbia* 'Nothowlee') **B**
- 3 pansies (*Viola* x *wittrockiana* 'Panola Deep Orange') **C**
- 3 variegated vincas (*Vinca minor* 'Illumination') **D**

Do you ever have a little spot that just needs a *pop* of fall color or need small pots to border some stairs? This part sun combination can be put together in about ten minutes once you gather all the ingredients. The euphorbia gets prettier as the autumn temperatures fall as its stems deepen to a burgundy red. The almost black leaves of the euphorbia combined with the orange pansies create a striking contrast against the chartreuse sweet flag grass. You'll find an echo of color with the trailing vinca vine as the chartreuse center and red stems brighten with colder weather too.

Here's the trick to keeping moisture loving *Acorus* looking good in this combination with more drought-tolerant plants: Cover the bottom half of the 1-gallon pot holding the *Acorus* grass with plastic wrap and lightly secure with a rubber band so that water escapes very slowly from that container. Then plant the entire pot with the *Acorus* grass into your container where indicated in the diagram. Surround everything with container mix potting soil and finish planting with the blackbird spurge, the pansies, and the vincas. Sweet flag is quite content with moist conditions so this will keep the grass looking good while the other plants get the drainage that they need to thrive. If the soil around the sweet flag gets too boggy, skip watering it for a few times and only water the plants surrounding it.

If you live in zones warmer than zone 6, this can also be used as a winter container. Fertilizing is generally *not* recommended for fall plantings except for a bloom-boosting fertilizer for the pansies once a month.

PLANT OPTIONS

All of these plants should be available in all hardiness zones. The euphorbia, with its unique coloring, will be sold in colder climates as a fall annual. For a look that has a more "Halloween" feel, substitute black mondo grass, Ophiopogon planiscapus, for the acorus grass.

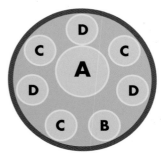

Lively Redhead

SUN PREFERENCE	CONTAINER SIZE	DIFFICULTY LEVEL
Full Sun	Large	Moderate

Shopping List

- Container mix potting soil
- 1 3-gallon-sized nandina (*Nandina domestica* 'Sienna Sunrise') **A**
- 3 1-gallon-sized false cypress (*Chamaecyparis pisifera* 'Golden Mop') **B**
- 6 pansies (*Viola* x *wittrockiana* 'Matrix Orange') **C**

Few plants provide the fall impact of color like the nandina bushes do. Going from the summertime subtle shades of green that just hint at vibrant coloring into a slow molting of yellows, orange, and red until it blazes a deep maroon red, this showstopper plant begs to be used in autumn containers. Paired with golden color of the false cypress and bright orange pansies, Lively Redhead will keep you mesmerized all season long.

With many of the larger plants that are used in this recipe book, I recommend aggressively trimming the diameter of the rootball of the plant. With the nandina, however, I've found that it doesn't respond well to having its roots being messed with. Gently just loosen the rootball and plant in the container where you've loosely poured the container mix potting soil. The *Chamaecyparis*, however, will need to have about an inch taken off the diameter and bottom of the rootball so that the plants can snuggle in close to each other. Finally, add the pansies as shown in the recipe diagram. It is worth mentioning that this full sun container recipe will not develop the rich array of color if it's put in a location that receives less than six hours of sunlight a day.

In zones 6 through 9, I've used this recipe for year-round containers, only exchanging the pansies in the spring with calibrachoa. Water requirements involve watering when the top of the soil is dry to touch. Fertilize the pansies once a month with a bloom-boosting plant food.

The nandina and false cypress are good plants to reuse in your landscape or to donate to your local Master Gardener programs to use in their volunteer landscaping projects.

PLANT OPTIONS

In some of the colder climates, nandina may be difficult to locate. A suitable substitute would be to use dwarf burning bush, Euonymus alatus *'Compactus'.*

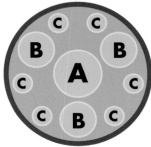

More Than Mums

Shopping List

- Container mix potting soil
- 1 2-gallon-sized croton (*Codiaeum* 'Petra') **A**
- 2 1-gallon-sized coral bells (*Heuchera* 'Plum Pudding') **B**
- 3 English ivies (*Hedera helix*) **C**
- 1 ornamental pepper (*Capsicum annuum*) **D**

Certain colors seem to be seasonal favorites. Red, green, silver, and gold for the winter, pastels in spring, maybe every bright color in summer, and orange and purple in fall. I was wandering around the indoor plants at a local nursery with an ornamental pepper in my hands when I noticed how the crotons wonderfully complemented the ornamental pepper. Morning sun, that unifying element that allows gardeners to combine more shade-loving plants with the more sun-loving plants, would be a perfect spot for the container recipe that I was designing in my mind. More Than Mums provides a display of fall colors and diverse textures that will provide a pleasant alternative to traditional autumn chrysanthemums.

The first plant that you should place in your container when making this recipe will be the croton, then position the other plants around the container according to the recipe diagram. This recipe was designed so that the container has a side that will be up against a wall, or it is positioned in some way that this back portion of the planter will not be highly visible. If you want to use this recipe in a location where the container will be viewed from all angles, you should add two more ornamental peppers and another ivy to the back part of the planter.

This recipe likes to be more on the dry side so only water when the top two inches of soil feel dry. The foliage on the crotons will be damaged if they experience a freeze so pull this planter indoors if a threat of freezing weather is imminent.

PLANT OPTIONS

You shouldn't have trouble finding these plants, but if you live in a zone where summers are mild and autumn freezes come early, this would be a good summertime planting to choose.

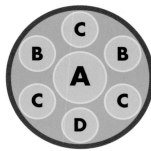

Refined Glory

SUN PREFERENCE	CONTAINER SIZE	DIFFICULTY LEVEL
Partial Sun	Large	Easy

Shopping List

- Container mix potting soil
- 3 1-gallon-sized variegated false hollies (*Osmanthus heterophyllus* 'Goshiki') **A**
- 1 5-gallon-sized red twig dogwood (*Cornus alba* 'Sibirica') **B**
- 3 black mondo grass (*Ophiopogon planiscapus* 'Nigrescens') **C**

Often when we're looking for a formal, more refined look in a container planting, our tendency is to use evergreens and topiaries. This recipe presents a well-maintained, controlled planting that is both refined and artistic. If you plant this recipe before the leaves of the dogwood fall off, know that the best is yet to come. The red branches of the dogwood intensify their color as the temperature cools off. The classic red, black, and white colors in these plants would be striking for an entryway or as a focal point in your landscape.

In this recipe you will need to center the red twig dogwood in the container before adding the remaining plants. When planting the black mondo grass, tilt the grass slightly toward the *outside* edge of the container to provide a spilling effect. This is an easy to maintain container recipe that involves little more than just making sure that the soil doesn't dry out in the planter. Both the red twig dogwood and the mondo grass like evenly moist, but not soggy, soil. Like several other fall container recipes, these plants can live through the winter in zones 6 and warmer, and could last for at least a year before outgrowing their container. Fertilize in the spring with a general-purpose plant food. Remember to gather the dogwood leaves that may fall on the lower part of the planting for a cleaner look to your container planting.

The plants in this recipe are wonderful plants to use in the landscape so think ahead of areas where you can reuse this combination. Check with your local Extension Service office or Habitat For Humanity to see if they know of projects needing landscape material.

Place a few white, red, and green Christmas decorations around the mondo grass and false hollies for a quick and simple holiday look.

PLANT OPTIONS

Variegated boxwood, Buxus *'Variegata', can be substituted in climates colder than zone 5 for the* Osmanthus, *but the red hues that the Osmanthus takes on as the temperatures drop will not be replicated in the boxwood.*

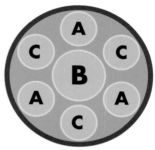

Rosemary and Red

SUN PREFERENCE	CONTAINER SIZE	DIFFICULTY LEVEL
Full Sun	Large	Easy

Shopping List

- Container mix potting soil
- 1 1-gallon-sized rosemary (*Rosmarinus officinalis* 'Arp') **A**
- 3 1-gallon-sized nandinas (*Nandina domestica* 'Firepower') **B**
- 3 bloodstone thrift (*Armeria maritima* 'Splendens') **C**
- 3 yellow pansies (*Viola* x *wittrockiana*) **D**
- 3 red pansies (*Viola* x *wittrockiana*) **E**

Yelena, a lady who has worked with me in the container gardening world for many years, inspires me with her many ideas. One of the best ideas that she uses in her fall plantings is to combine rosemary with her perennial and annual containers. For years I had made rosemary a staple in my container herb plantings, but after seeing Yelena's creative combinations using the aromatic and evergreen (in zones 6 and warmer) herb, I decided to start using rosemary more artistically also.

The intensifying red of the nandina and the opportunity to use rosemary in many fall stews and cooking recipes is the prompt behind presenting this as a fall container recipe. In zones 6 and warmer this recipe could even be used as a winter planting. In many areas fall is one of

the driest times of the year, so this water-wise planting will be happy in the cooling, drier days of autumn.

Center the rosemary in the container before proceeding with planting the remainder of the recipe's ingredients. When positioning the nandina and *Armeria*, tilt the plants slightly toward the outside rim of the container. Often when planting at an angle, part of the rootball can stick up above the potting soil in the container. Gently use your hands or a gardening trowel to cut back the rootball so that it will still be covered with soil when the container is watered.

Water only when the top of the soil is dry to your touch and be careful not to overwater. Fertilize the pansies once a month with a liquid bloom-boosting plant food.

PLANT OPTIONS

There are not any plants that are unusual in this container recipe. In some areas, it can even be a winter container planting.

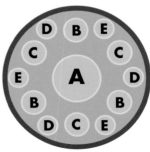

Royal Gold

SUN PREFERENCE	CONTAINER SIZE	DIFFICULTY LEVEL
Full Sun	Medium	Easy

Shopping List

- Container mix potting soil
- 1 1-gallon-sized cypress (*Cupressus macrocarpa* 'Gold Crest') **A**
- 3 1-gallon-sized longleaf pines (*Pinus palustris*) **B**
- 3 ornamental kale (*Brassica oleracea*) **C**
- 3 purple pansies (*Viola* x *wittrockiana*) **D**

This recipe actually contains several of the same plants as the Yellow and White Mix-Up recipe but I wanted to show how different a container can look using similar plants that are simply smaller and varied in position. A younger tree or shrub can sometimes have either a more intense or a muted coloring, or may have a shape that will just work better in a smaller container.

Begin by placing the cypress in middle of the container in loosely poured container mix potting soil. Next, plant the longleaf pines, then the kale, with each of them at a slight angle where they are facing the outside edge of the container. While these are not trailing type plants, this slight tilt toward the edge will help give a more finished touch to the planting.

If you live in a climate that rarely has frost, the kale may attempt to start blooming. Although their flower is very pretty, I recommend keeping the blooms pinched back because they will get quite tall, throwing the design of the recipe off balance.

This recipe has low water requirements after the pansies and kale have rooted in, which usually takes two or three weeks. After these annuals have become established, water only when the top two inches of soil have dried out. If you see the pansies start to wilt, it's time for a nice long drink of water for your planting! Too much water will cause the pansies and kale to rot or to develop problems with disease. Use a bloom-boosting fertilizer once a month around the pansies and kale.

Both ornamental kale and pansies are edible (as long as they have not been sprayed). The purple pansies from this container recipe can be candied or used as a festive garnish for fall holiday events.

PLANT OPTIONS

You should be able to find all the plants in this recipe pretty easily. But, Thuja 'Aurea Nana' is a good option to use if the cypress cannot be found.

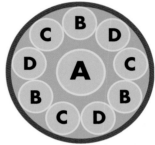

Russian Hat

SUN PREFERENCE	CONTAINER SIZE	DIFFICULTY LEVEL
Full Sun	**Medium**	**Easy**

Shopping List

- Container mix potting soil
- 1 1-gallon-sized thread-branch false cypress (*Chamaecyparis pisifera filifera* 'Sungold') **A**
- 3 stonecrops (*Sedum spurium* 'Dragon's Blood') **B**
- 6 trailing violas (*Viola* hybrid 'Purple Rain') **C**

Russian Hat combines two of my favorite elements in container planting: ease of care and a great new plant cultivar. There are several cultivars of trailing violas and this one, *Viola* 'Purple Rain', proved itself faithfully. As far as ease of care, the planter where I first planted this recipe was in a difficult to reach, full-sun location and the dependability on it getting watered properly was minimal. In spite of all that, Russian Hat performed well all autumn. This recipe actually thrives throughout the winter in my zone 6 location, as it would in most areas in zones 5 through 10. In the warmer areas, the maintenance requirements will increase with a need for more frequent watering.

The *Chamaecyparis* will need to be planted first when you are putting this container together. Be careful *not* to plant the rootball too low in the planter so you have room to plant the remaining plants without the violas and *Sedum* getting squished. Water only when the top 2 to 3 inches of soil are dry. If you see the violas looking droopy, that is your indication that this recipe needs water. However, always check the soil *before* you water—sometimes the violas can look droopy after heavy rains or a frost and water is *not* what is needed!

Violas are heavy feeders and you should feed them once a month with a liquid bloom-boosting fertilizer. The trick here will be to feed the violas *without* getting much on the *Sedum*, which does not like to be regularly fertilized. There are several granular pansy- and viola-specific fertilizers that, if you can find them, you should use instead of the liquid fertilizers; just sprinkle it around the soil underneath your violas.

PLANT OPTIONS

Gold Coast® juniper (Juniperus x pfitzeriana 'Aurea Improved') might be an easier plant to find than the Chamaecyparis 'Sungold' across the diverse zones, and it will offer a similar look to this recipe.

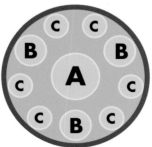

A Subtle Welcome

Shopping List

- Container mix potting soil
- 1 5-gallon-sized dwarf golden arborvitae (*Thuja orientalis* 'Aurea nana') **A**
- 1 2-gallon-sized autumn fern (*Dryopteris erythrosora*) **B**
- 2 1-gallon-sized sweet flag grass (*Acorus gramineus* 'Ogon') **C**
- 1 1-gallon-sized coral bells (*Heuchera* 'Crimson Curls') **D**
- 2 1-gallon-sized variegated ivies (*Hedera helix* 'Gold Child') **E**

Who needs flowers when foliage can be so interesting? Full and frilly autumn fern is an attention getter on its own. But combined here with flowing ivies, spikey sweet flag grass, a neat mound of *Heuchera*, and with the solid background of a *Thuja orientalis*, this planting always gets compliments. *Acorus*, commonly called sweet flag, derived its name because of the sweet fragrance that is emitted whenever the blades are pressed or crushed. When this large planter is placed next to a doorway, a gentle brushing past can sweeten up your entrance.

Several of these plants, such as the *Thuja orientalis* and ivies, can tolerate dry conditions but sweet flag grass and autumn fern like to stay evenly moist so keep this planting well watered without being soggy. This is best done by watering only when the top of the soil feels dry to your touch.

To keep this looking attractive year-round, trim back any tired looking foliage on the autumn fern and coral bells in early spring. Also, feed with a general-purpose fertilizer in early spring and midsummer.

With a recipe that calls for a plant that has a rootball larger than the other plants, shave off about an inch around the diameter of the rootball and place first in your large container. Next, position the autumn fern and sweet flag according to the recipe diagram. When planting the *Heuchera* and ivies tilt the plants slightly toward the outside of the pot. Add any additional soil that may be needed to fill in spaces between plants. Then lightly brush the sweet flag and take a deep breath—*mmmm!*

PLANT OPTIONS

All of these plants should be available in every hardiness zone for fall containers. But in zones 6 and warmer, all of these plants are evergreen, and would also make nice winter or even year-round plantings in those areas.

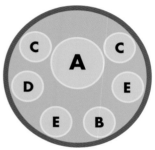

Sweet Winter Roses

SUN PREFERENCE	CONTAINER SIZE	DIFFICULTY LEVEL
Shade	Large	Easy

Shopping List

- Container mix potting soil
- 2 Tbs. used coffee grounds
- 1 5-gallon-sized camellia (*Camellia* 'Winter's Joy') **A**
- 2 1-gallon-sized honeysuckles (*Lonicera nitida* 'Edmee Gold') **B**
- 4 periwinkles (*Vinca minor* 'Illumination') **C**
- 1 1-gallon-sized coral bells (*Heuchera* hybrid 'Mahogany') **D**

This recipe ranks as one of my all-time favorites. Maybe it's the memory of camellias blooming under my bedroom window or the bowl of what my grandmamma called "winter roses," her name for camellias, that decorated our Thanksgiving table, but this recipe always makes me happy and is repeated in at least one container every autumn. If camellias are hard to find in your area, this is one plant that I would recommend ordering through the mail and making the effort to winter over indoors. In areas warmer than zone 6, this recipe can be maintained for several years in the same container as long as it has adequate water and fertilizing.

When putting together a container recipe that calls for a large accent plant such as this five-gallon-sized camellia, only fill your container a little over halfway full of container mix potting soil. This way it is easier to position the camellia correctly in the planter. Before placing the camellia in the container, sprinkle the used coffee grounds on top of the potting mix where the camellia will be planted. Camellias are happiest and bloom best in acidic soil and this bit of coffee grounds helps give the soil below the camellia a lower pH without adversely affecting the remaining plants. Add additional container mix once the camellia is centered and continue planting, placing the *Lonicera* and *Heuchera* according to the recipe diagram. Finish by planting the periwinkles.

Water when the top of the surface is dry to your touch. If you are keeping this planting over the winter, fertilize with a general-purpose fertilizer in the early spring.

PLANT OPTIONS

There is not much that can be substituted in this recipe other than using different cultivars for the Heuchera, Lonicera, *and camellia. The Ice Angel® camellias have a wonderful reputation for their cold hardiness through zone 6.*

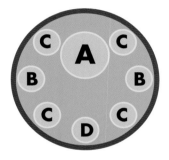

Whimsical Blues

SUN PREFERENCE	CONTAINER SIZE	DIFFICULTY LEVEL
Full Sun	Medium	Easy

Shopping List

- Container mix potting soil
- 1 3-gallon-sized blue cedar (*Cedrus deodara* 'Feelin' Blue') **A**
- 3 4-inch pot dwarf sweet flag grass (*Acorus gramineus* 'Minimus Aureus') **B**
- 3 4-inch pot nandinas (*Nandina domestica* 'Firepower') **C**

My daddy once told me that one of the healthiest things I could do in life is not take myself too seriously. He worked his whole life in the forestry industry and I think that he would have *loved* it that this blue cedar seems to fit in a category of plants that just might not take themselves too seriously. The whimsy and free-form artistry of the *Cedrus deodara* 'Feelin' Blue' will create an interesting display in your container.

After loosely filling your planter about three-fourths full of the container mix, plant the cedar first, centering it according to the recipe diagram. Then add potting mix as needed to hold the rootball in place, with enough room left in the container to plant the *Acorus* and nandinas. Slightly tilt the *Acorus* and nandinas toward the edge of the container to help them look like they are spilling over the edge of the planter. Make sure to cover any exposed roots that poke up when these plants are tilted with more mix.

Maintaining an evenly moist soil will be your biggest challenge with this recipe combination. The *Acorus* does not like to dry out but neither the nandinas nor the cedar want to sit in soggy soil. Water when the top of the soil is dry to your touch.

As the temperatures cool down in the fall, you'll be delighted with the fiery red colors that these nandinas display. Contrasted with the blue tones of the cedar and the chartreuse of the sweet flag grass, this planting will provide some serious fall color. And whimsy.

Use miniature white lights on the blue cedar during the holidays for an easy transition into a holiday planter.

PLANT OPTIONS

If you have difficulty locating this exact Cedrus *species and cultivar, look for any three-gallon-sized evergreen plant that looks like it might have come from a Dr. Seuss children's book. You can't go wrong.*

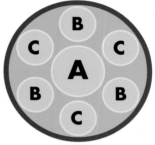

Wine Punch

SUN PREFERENCE
Partial Sun

CONTAINER SIZE
Large

DIFFICULTY LEVEL
Easy

Shopping List

- Container mix potting soil
- 1 3-gallon-sized 'Ever Red'® fringe flower (*Loropetalum chinense* 'Chang Nian Hong') **A**
- 2 1-gallon-sized 'Blue Creeper'® junipers (*Juniperus scopulorum* 'Monam') **B**
- 3 stonecrops (*Sedum reflexum* 'Angelina') **C**

Some folks may scratch their heads when they see this recipe listed as a fall planting because they are probably thinking about *Loropetalum* being a spring-flowering shrub. And you can surely plant this in the spring to enjoy the flowers. This shrub, however, can produce a sporadic fall flush of flowers. But what I enjoy using this plant for is the dark burgundy foliage that complements the surrounding fall colors. Paired with the icy blue foliage of the juniper and contrasting to the chartreuse *Sedum* 'Angelina', this is a very simple planting that packs a lot of punch.

In this container recipe, begin by centering the *Loropetalum* in your container. *Loropetalum* doesn't like having anyone mess with its root

systems so only use your hands to *gently* loosen a few roots. Add more soil around the rootball while still leaving room to plant the juniper and *Sedum*. This cultivar of sedum takes on a bronzy red blush of color as the temperatures start to cool off that blends well with the foliage of the fringe flower. For a blast of early spring color if you're wintering over in the milder zones, plant a dozen yellow crocus bulbs around the edge of this planting.

Water this container recipe when the top of the soil is dry to your touch. In zones 7 through zone 9, this recipe can be used as a year-round planting. The folks in those zones who want to maintain these throughout the year should fertilize in the early spring and late summer with a general-purpose fertilizer.

PLANT OPTIONS

There is not much that could be substituted for the Loropetalum *that has similar leaf structure and shape. But for those in zones 3 and warmer,* Sambucus *'Black Lace' provides a similar color option that is much more cold hardy. There are quite a few cultivar options for substitutions for the* Loropetalum, *such as 'Sizzling Pink' and 'Zhuzhou Fuschia', and for the juniper, such as 'Wiltonii' or 'Blue Star'.*

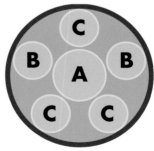

Wispy Window Box

SUN PREFERENCE	CONTAINER SIZE	DIFFICULTY LEVEL
Partial Sun	**Small**	**Easy**

Shopping List

- Container mix potting soil
- 2 1-gallon-sized sweet flag grass (*Acorus gramineus* 'Ogon') **A**
- 1 1-gallon-sized coral bells (*Heuchera* 'Black Beauty') **B**
- 2 pansies (*Viola* x *wittrockiana* 'Panola Pink Shade') **C**
- 4 1-quart-sized miniature moss false cypress (*Chamaecyparis pisifera* 'Squarrosa minima')

This recipe remains a favorite of mine for two reasons: the look of joy on the owner's face when he saw what his long-empty window box could look like, and my own look of amazement at seeing how wonderful this recipe looked six months later when I came by to replant it with spring annuals. In the fall, part-sun plantings of sweet flag grass and the many cultivars of *Heuchera* are hard to beat as dependable container plants. And as container gardening explodes in popularity, the availability of quart-sized miniature shrubs—not to be confused with the more expensive bonsai plants—will make planting year-round window boxes much simpler and easier.

Window boxes can be a little tricky when planting, depending on their location at a house. I usually only fill the boxes halfway with container mix potting soil when I am using one-gallon-sized plants. Begin planting by placing the plants that are farthest away from where you are positioned. In this example shown by the photo, I was standing outside the house in front of the window box so I started by planting one of the *Chamaecyparis* in each end of the box. Next I planted the *Acorus* and *Heuchera*, tilting the *Heuchera* toward the outside edge of the window box. Then the two remaining *Chamaecyparis* were planted, followed by the pansies. Fill in any gaps around the plants with more potting soil.

Keep this recipe evenly moist by watering when the top of the soil feels dry to your touch. In this part-sun location, the pansies may tend to stretch and get "leggy" looking. Pinch the pansies back to about 4 inches to encourage them to branch and bloom. Use a general-purpose fertilizer in the early spring if wintering this recipe over in areas warmer than zone 4.

PLANT OPTIONS

If the miniature-sized Chamaecyparis *are difficult to find, a similar look can be found by using* Sedum *'John Creech'.*

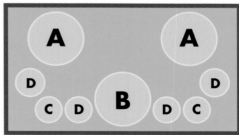

Yellow and White Mix-Up

SUN PREFERENCE	CONTAINER SIZE	DIFFICULTY LEVEL
Full Sun	Extra Large	Moderate

Shopping List

- Container mix potting soil
- 1 5-gallon-sized cypress (*Cupressus macrocarpa* 'Gold Crest') **A**
- 1 1-gallon-sized longleaf pine (*Pinus palustris*) **B**
- 1 ornamental kale (*Brassica oleracea* 'White Feather') **C**
- 1 dusty miller (*Senecio cineraria* 'Dusty Miller') **D**
- 2 parsley plants (*Petroselinum crispum*) **E**
- 1 lemongrass (*Cymbopogon citratus*) **F**
- 3 yellow violas (*Viola* x *wittrockiana*) **G**

On one of my regular road trips to haunt the greenhouses of Saul Nurseries in Atlanta, Georgia, I saw this container planting and heard that tiny voice in my head that said, "This is recipe worth repeating." (The *other* little voice . . .) Fortunately, Bobby Saul graciously shares his container recipes so we all can enjoy the beauty of this combination at our own homes. I like how the red tones of the cypress branches peek out through the glowing yellow, how the lemongrass blades are mingled through the other plants in different directions, and the echo of yellow and white throughout the recipe.

Before planting the cypress in your container, use the edge of a trowel or a hori-hori knife (a *great* Japanese style knife with a serrated edge) to trim off about 2 inches around the diameter of the cypress rootball. With a rootball this large,

make sure that the container mix potting soil has only filled a little over half of the planter; otherwise, there won't be room for all the plants. It is easier to add more soil if the plants are sitting too low in the container than it is to remove the excess soil. After positioning the cypress as shown by the recipe diagram, add more soil for planting the remaining plants. Plant the longleaf pine, kale, and parsley as the diagram indicates, then finish with the dusty miller, lemongrass, and the violas. Carefully weave a few strands of the lemongrass through the violas as your finishing touch.

Extra-large containers can often be easier to maintain because there is more potting mix for holding water. Water only when the top 2 or 3 inches of soil feel dry. Fertilize the violas once a month with a bloom-boosting fertilizer.

PLANT OPTIONS

*'Aurea nana' is a good
substitute for the cypress.
You may have to hunt a bit
for the longleaf pine.*

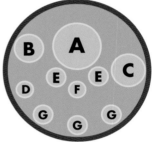

WINTER

Black and Tan

SUN PREFERENCE	CONTAINER SIZE	DIFFICULTY LEVEL
Partial Sun	Large	Easy

SHOPPING LIST

- Container mix potting soil
- Sheet moss
- 1 3-gallon-sized fernspray false cypress (*Chamaecyparis obtusa* 'Filicoides') **A**
- 5 1-gallon-sized coral bells (*Heuchera villosa* 'Caramel') **B**
- 5 black mondo grass (*Ophiopogon planiscapus* 'Nigrescens') **C**
- 5 English ivies (*Hedera helix*) **D**

There are a few plantings that seem to be everyone's favorite—they're not too flashy, often quite simple, and there seems to be a quirky welcoming quality about them. This planting falls into that category. Whenever I put this combination together, folks just seem to be satisfied with the results.

Maybe the appeal is the odd imperfection of the fernspray false cypress, its random twists and turns that give it an informal air. Or it could be the warm colors of the 'Caramel' coral bells and their big, soft-looking round leaves. Mix in the little tufts of black mondo grass and good old-fashioned English ivy, and the combo just *clicks*.

Even though this planting can handle full sun in areas from zone 5 to colder, I've listed this as only partial sun, especially once you get into zone 6 and the warmer zones. 'Caramel' is one of the few *Heuchera* cultivars that can handle

both the cold and heat but it does not like afternoon southern sun. You'll enjoy how the winter color of the English ivy with its reddish stems blends so well with the apricot tones that the *Heuchera* takes on. All of these plants are happy in containers and are easy to grow in the same large planter for several years. You may need to trim the ivies if they start growing into the soil below the planter. You should also trim the dead summer flowers off the *Heuchera* to maintain a tidy look.

This container recipe is easy to maintain. The plants all like a spot of water throughout the winter only when the soil on the surface is dry to the touch. This planting has a layer of moss around the edge to give the planting a finished look where soil was exposed. This is also a good way to keep moisture in the soil and protect the roots of your container plants.

PLANT OPTIONS

This is one of the few recipes where there really aren't plant substitutions. You need to find these plants in order to achieve this look.

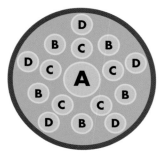

Blue Spruce Holiday

SUN PREFERENCE	CONTAINER SIZE	DIFFICULTY LEVEL
Full Sun	Extra Large	Easy

Shopping List

- Container mix potting soil
- 1 5-gallon-sized blue spruce (*Picea pungens glauca* 'Fat Albert') **A**
- 5 nandinas (*Nandina domestica* 'Firepower') **B**
- 5 yuccas (*Yucca* 'Color Guard') **C**

I put together this sun-loving planter for a friend who wanted "something she wouldn't have to think about very often." This nandina cultivar has one of the longest lasting and most intensely red colors of any nandina that I've worked with. It stays compact and mounding, making it a wonderful little edging inside a large planter. The yucca variety used in this container planting also has long lasting intense color, with the yellow in the leaves brightening throughout the winter and even taking on a pink tinge in the coldest temperatures. If you have shied away from using yuccas in the past due to their mean old spikey leaves, you'll be pleasantly surprised by the gentleness of this yucca's leaves.

The texture and color combinations are very appealing. The blue-green stripe along the yucca's leaves coordinate nicely with the blue spruce. The brilliant red of the nandina looks almost like decorations ready to be placed among the spruce's branches. The nandina's soft oval leaves contrast nicely with the stiff spruce needles. The yucca, with its long yellow leaves, breaks up the heaviness of the spruce needles and tight mound of the nandina. For a festive event you could wrap lights around the branches of the spruce.

Each of these three types of plants are slow growing and need little to no pruning, so they could easily live in this planter for several years as long as they were maintained properly. Very low maintenance, this planter needs watering only when the top two inches of soil are dry to the touch and fertilizing with a general-purpose fertilizer in early spring and midsummer. The yucca may bloom in spring with a fragrant white flower; you should prune back the stem after the bloom has died. The spruce is happier in cooler climates so make sure this planting gets some protection from the hot afternoon sun if you live south of the Mason-Dixon line and are maintaining this planting year-round.

PLANT OPTIONS

In areas colder than zone 5, the nandina could be substituted by Sedum spurium *'Bronze Carpet'.*

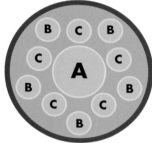

Colorful Winter Punch

SUN PREFERENCE	CONTAINER SIZE	DIFFICULTY LEVEL
Partial Sun	Medium	Easy

Shopping List

- Container mix potting soil
- 2 2-gallon-sized variegated boxwoods (*Buxus sempervirens* 'Variegata') **A**
- 1 2-gallon-sized arborvitae (*Thuja occidentalis* 'Yellow Ribbon') **B**
- 5 black mondo grass (*Ophiopogon planiscapus* 'Nigrescens') **C**
- 7 wine-colored pansies (*Viola* x *wittrockiana*) **D**

Snuggle these plants together to create a winter deck box planting with some *punch*! Rectangular or deck box containers are useful for creating a border along a porch or for creating a small "room" in your garden. While putting these shrubs so close together isn't something I recommend for long-term landscape use, this combination for a winter container offers a nice wall of color for the winter months.

When planting the shrubs next to one another, shave off at least an inch of soil around their rootballs so that the plants can fit closely together. First plant the three shrubs in the container before adding the remaining plants called for in the recipe. The black mondo grass is a nice way to soften the edges of a planting.

For this planting you need to be aware of where the sun hits the container. Remember that when a planting will be seen from both the front and the back, one side may not be getting as much sun. In the placement of the planter in *this* picture, only the front of the planter gets morning sun so only the more shade-tolerant black mondo grass should be used along the back under the three shrubs. If pansies were planted in that spot, they would tend to get leggy quickly trying to reach for sunlight. They also would not flower as much. Keep this in mind when reviewing the diagram because it was created for the particular location of this planter, and the sun that it receives.

All the plants in Colorful Winter Punch are drought tolerant and easy to care for. The shrubs would be wonderful replanted in a landscape or used again in a larger container where they could be used individually as a focal point in another combination.

PLANT OPTIONS

*You should be able to find the plants in
this recipe. They are needed to duplicate
this look.*

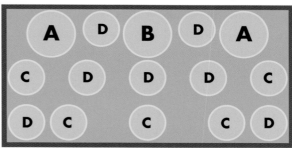

Cool Winter Pine

SUN PREFERENCE	CONTAINER SIZE	DIFFICULTY LEVEL
Full Sun	Large	Easy

Shopping List

- Container mix potting soil
- 1 5-gallon-sized white pine (*Pinus parviflora* 'Blue Angel') **A**
- 1 1-gallon-sized sedum (*Sedum spurium* 'Bronze Carpet') **B**
- 3 1-gallon-sized coral bells (*Heuchera* 'Fire Chief') **C**
- 5 pansies (*Viola* x *wittrockiana* 'True Blue') **D**

Do you like the idea of angels guarding your door? This planting with the 'Blue Angel' white pine is a heavenly combination of blues and reds. I have rarely seen an evergreen with such a strong tone of blue as the 'Blue Angel' white pine. The branches on the pine look like puffballs, creating almost a whimsical look. The addition of 'True Blue' pansies carries on the blue theme among the lower plantings.

Contrasting both in textures and colors with the stiff pine needles are the large, soft, round *Heuchera* leaves. The 'Fire Chief' variety deepens to a fiery wine red color throughout the winter. This *Heuchera* is also one of the varieties that bloom from spring until fall so you'll have red-stemmed pink-and-white flowers throughout the growing season. Spilling out the front of the container is an evergreen *Sedum* called 'Bronze Carpet', which repeats the coral bells' coloring.

When putting this recipe together in your container, plant the large pine first so that it can be centered and set so that it is not leaning one way or the other. Next add the *Heuchera* and *Sedum* as they are shown on the recipe diagram. Finally, plant the pansies, tilting them slightly toward the outside of the container so they will begin to spill over the edge.

This is another container planting that prefers to be on the dry side so allow the soil to dry out between waterings. This pine only grows to about 7 to 8 feet, so you could easily leave this combination in a large container for years. Just replace the pansies in the late spring with blue *Scaevola* or blue *Calibrachoa* to continue to reflect the blue tones of the pine. These annuals will last through the summer until the first frost, where you can replace them once again with 'True Blue' pansies. Keep this planting fed throughout the year with a 10-10-10 granular fertilizer and fertilize your pansies and summer flowers once a month with a bloom-boosting liquid fertilizer.

PLANT OPTIONS

A comparable substitute for Sedum 'Bronze Carpet' would be 'Dragon's Blood' or 'Voodoo'. Of course, these variety names don't sound like good companions to a 'Blue Angel'!

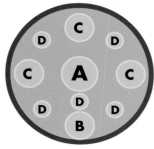

Dazzling Tiny White Flowers

SUN PREFERENCE	CONTAINER SIZE	DIFFICULTY LEVEL
Shade	Medium	Easy

Shopping List

- Container mix potting soil
- 1 3-gallon-sized lily-of-the-valley shrub (*Pieris japonica* 'Mountain Fire') **A**
- 3 1-gallon-sized Japanese sedges (*Carex hachijoensis* 'Evergold') **B**
- 2 1-gallon-sized coral bells (*Heuchera micrantha* 'Palace Purple') **C**

Prepare to be dazzled by the new spring growth on this combination. Draping white miniature flower bells cover the *Pieris japonica* 'Mountain Fire' along with its deep red new leaf growth. *Heuchera* 'Palace Purple' will burst with tall towers of creamy white tiny flowers by mid-spring and last through early summer. With the soft draping of the 'Evergold' Japanese sedge, this spring planting will provide an interesting array of subtle colors and textures to accent a north-facing doorway or a shaded garden spot.

In zones 6b and warmer, plant this during the fall to use as a winter and early spring container planting since all three plant types remain evergreen during these colder months. Because these plants will not get a whole lot larger than what is planted, this combination is also a good choice for a year-round planting. If you keep this planting in the same container for several years, remember to fertilize in early spring and midsummer with a general-purpose fertilizer. While this is generally a shade-loving combination, this planting can handle several hours of morning sun. Keep this planting evenly moist—you don't want the soil to dry out completely. The leaves of the *Pieris japonica* are a good indicator of when your soil is too dry: They will droop slightly to get your attention when they are thirsty plants!

Snip off a little of the *Pieris japonica* to add to your cut flower arrangements or to use in a centerpiece. Its glossy leaves are great accents to arrangements.

PLANT OPTIONS

If you prefer it, Heuchera *'Amethyst Mist' can be substituted for 'Palace Purple'. But 'Palace Purple' should be available just about everywhere.*

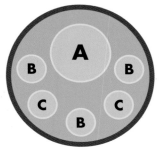

Evergreen, Ever Pretty

SUN PREFERENCE	CONTAINER SIZE	DIFFICULTY LEVEL
Partial Sun	Medium	Easy

Shopping List

- Container mix potting soil
- ⅛ tsp. moisture control pellets such as Soil Moist®
- 1 1-gallon-sized black pine (*Pinus nigra*) **A**
- 1 1-gallon-sized coral bells (*Heuchera* 'Amethyst Mist') **B**
- 1 1-gallon-sized variegated Japanese sedge (*Carex morrowii*) **C**

Leonardo da Vinci supposedly said that simplicity is the ultimate sophistication. This little trio is about as simple to put together and maintain as planting combos come, yet it will provide you with classic sophistication throughout winter. Exemplifying the standard "thriller, filler, and spiller" mantra of container gardening, the black pine is the thriller, the *Heuchera* is the filler, and the *Carex* acts as the spiller. Plant the black pine first when putting this recipe together, followed by the coral bells, then the Japanese sedge. When planting the *Carex,* turn the plant to a slight angle as you plant to enhance the spiller effect.

Since the variegated Japanese sedge does best when it stays evenly moist, place the moisture control pellets underneath it. (If you are having a hard time finding moisture control pellets, place a small square of thin sponge—about an inch is all you need—to help retain water near the roots of the *Carex*.) Once you've gotten a source for extra moisture positioned around your Japanese sedge, water this planter when the top of the soil is dry to your touch.

The black pine is a moderate grower so you won't want to keep these plants in this size planter for more than a year. When planting this recipe, be thinking of where you can locate these plants in your landscape after you remove them the following season.

All of the plants in this recipe are good ones to reuse in your landscape or to donate to your local Master Gardener program to use in any of their volunteer landscaping projects.

PLANT OPTIONS

Two other pines that could be more available in your area are the shore pine, Pinus contorta, *or* Pinus flexilis *'Vanderwolf's Pyramid'.*

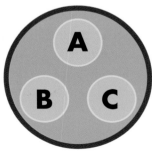

Jump Ups and Shout

SUN PREFERENCE	CONTAINER SIZE	DIFFICULTY LEVEL
Full Sun	Large	Easy

Shopping List

- Container mix potting soil
- 3 1-gallon-sized blue juniper (*Juniperus scopulorum* 'Witchita Blue') **A**
- 3 6-inch-diameter pots golden pincushion false cypress (*Chamaecyparis pisifera* 'Golden Pincushion') **B**
- 4 6-inch-diameter pots variegated boxwood (*Buxus sempervirens*) **C**
- 10 violas (*Viola cornuta* 'Denim Jump Up') **D**
- 6 red pansies (*Viola* x *wittrockiana*) **E**

The clients for whom I planted this combination wanted a winter container that would draw attention away from the defoliated winter landscape that flanked their walkway up to their home. Not only did this colorful assortment grab a visitor's attention, the height of the 'Witchita Blue' junipers worked to block the carpet rose branches that lay starkly behind them. It was a delight to see this planting used for three more years at this location before the plants outgrew their container. In the late spring we replaced the pansies and violas with blue and red calibrachoa, but the containers had a little more competition for attention when the carpet roses resumed blooming in the landscape. Fall brought back a planting of violas and pansies to replace the summer annuals in the container. With a matching container across the walkway, this container recipe provided a welcoming boundary in their rectangular planters.

When planting this combination, place the three 'Witchita Blue' junipers first to establish even spacing in the planter. Next, add the variegated boxwoods along what will be the "back" of the planting. Place the *Chamaecyparis* 'Golden Pincushion'—which is sometimes called golden false cypress—in the locations specified by the recipe. Finish by filling in the spaces with the violas and pansies.

If this planting is being used where the back side of the planter is up against a wall or fence, you can save a little on cost by eliminating the variegated boxwoods and pansies planted along the back of the planting. The 'Witchita Blue' juniper is very cold tolerant, making this one of the most cold hardy of these winter recipes. It's also drought resistant, a bonus in today's world.

PLANT OPTIONS

If needed, you can substitute Sedum *'Angelina'*
if the golden pincushion false cypress is difficult
to locate.

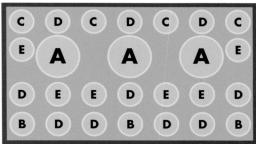

The King and His Court

SUN PREFERENCE	CONTAINER SIZE	DIFFICULTY LEVEL
Full Sun	Large	Easy

Shopping List

- Container mix potting soil
- 1 5-gallon-sized Japanese black pine (*Pinus thunbergiana*) **A**
- 8 6-inch-sized variegated boxwood (*Buxus sempervirens*) **B**
- 8 English ivies (*Hedera helix*) **C**
- 8 purple pansies (*Viola* x *wittrockiana*) **D**

Simple and elegant, this container planting is about easy care and classic beauty. This full-sun planting can take some shade, but in either location the water requirements are small. These plants like the soil to dry out between plantings but don't *totally* forget about them! Pansies are not always a good indicator plant for watering because they can droop due to freezing weather, too little water, or even from too much water. Be willing to stick your finger into the dirt about an inch and only water if the soil is dry.

The Japanese black pine will be the first plant that you'll put in your container as you start preparing this recipe. Remember to only fill the container halfway with container mix potting soil before placing the black pine in the planter. Then, before placing the boxwoods in the planter you may need to add more potting soil around the rootball of the black pine. Boxwoods are very slow growing so using them in planters is a good way to save a little money by letting them grow for several years until they reach a more acceptable landscaping size.

In this planting the ivies and Japanese black pine will grow too quickly to keep this planting for more than a year, and the pansies would also need to be replanted in the late spring with summer annuals like purple calibrachoa. The Japanese black pine can eventually grow to over 50 feet high and 25 feet wide so think of a good spot to transplant this in your landscape. When you are ready to replant this container for a new season, the black pine is a good tree to donate to projects that may need trees for screening, like a local school or park. At this point you can continue using the boxwoods for container plantings to allow them more time to grow, or plant them directly in the ground also.

During the winter, keep your pansies fed with a liquid fertilizer to encourage new blooms. Pansies can be pinched back to about 6 inches during the late winter, early spring season to encourage a fuller look.

PLANT OPTIONS

Two other pines that might be more available in different areas are the shore pine, Pinus contorta, *or* Pinus flexilis *'Vanderwolf's Pyramid'.*

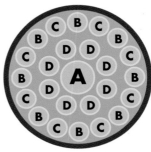

Rosy Color Guard

SUN PREFERENCE	CONTAINER SIZE	DIFFICULTY LEVEL
Full Sun	Medium	Easy

Shopping List

- Container mix potting soil
- 1 1-gallon-sized wintercreeper (*Euonymus fortunei* 'Emerald Gaiety') **A**
- 3 miniature moss false cypress (*Chamaecyparis pisifera* 'Squarrosa minima') **B**
- 3 English ivies (*Hedera helix*) **C**
- 6 rose-colored pansies (*Viola* x *wittrockiana*) **D**

Here's a sun-loving little winter recipe that will keep your attention throughout the cold season. This *Euonymus* variety responds like a rosy-cheeked child to the cold, taking on a beautiful blush of red to its gold-edged leaves as the temperatures fall. But even before the cooler weather takes hold, this planter provides a vibrant look of gold and rosy-red with the addition of rose-colored pansies.

Textural interest is provided by adding compact little balls of the miniature moss false cypress that contrast well with the open branches of the *Euonymus*, the large leaves of the ivies, and the big, colorful pansy heads. Cohesiveness is brought to the planting with complementary rosy tones in the pansies, *Euonymus*, and the winter color of the ivy stems. Plant the wintercreeper first in a medium-sized container, then proceed with planting the smaller plants as shown in the recipe diagram.

Another easy to maintain container, this recipe needs regular watering but keep the soil on the dry side or the pansies could develop mildew on their leaves. Pinch back the pansy heads to prevent them from getting too leggy throughout the season and give them some liquid bloom-boosting fertilizer once a month to encourage new blooms. Don't be alarmed if your pansies look lethargic during cold temperatures; they will bounce back once the air starts warming up.

PLANT OPTIONS

Euonymus fortunei *'Ivory Jade'* is a similar cultivar that can be use that is a little more cold hardy than the *'Emerald Gaiety'*, which is only hardy through zone 5. Sedum reflexum *'Blue Spruce'* is found from zones 3 to 11 and could be substituted for the miniature moss false cypress.

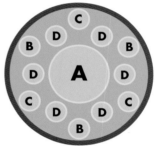

Southern Belle

SUN PREFERENCE	CONTAINER SIZE	DIFFICULTY LEVEL
Shade	Medium	Easy

Shopping List

- Container mix potting soil
- 3 1-gallon-sized camellias (*Camellia japonica* 'Spring's Promise Ice Angel®') **A**
- 2 1-gallon-sized coral bells (*Heuchera* 'Obsidian') **B**
- 1 1-gallon-sized bush honeysuckle (*Lonicera* 'Edmee Gold') **C**

I have to admit that this is one of my favorite winter plantings. Maybe it's my southern roots that associate winter-blooming camellias with fun holiday gatherings but this simple container recipe always makes me happy. Those who live in zones colder than zone 6 will fuss about me calling this a winter planting because camellias won't live through the winters there. But just shuffle this planting idea over to an autumn or early springtime container recipe where the camellia will bring you roselike blossoms long before your roses even *think* of blooming.

These three evergreen plants, for those in zone 6 and warmer, allow some bright color in your shady areas. Even when the 'Spring's Promise' camellias are not blooming, the 'Edmee Gold' honeysuckle is lighting up the container with its chartreuse color. Even in warmer climates the more cold hardy camellias do better in containers. Also remember that depending on the variety, camellias can bloom anytime from early fall to late spring.

Place the camellias first in your planter to establish proper spacing in your container, then plant the 'Obsidian' coral bells slightly angled toward the front corners of the rectangular planter. Finally, nestle the 'Edmee Gold' honeysuckle between the two *Heuchera* plants and fill in any gaps between the root systems of the plants with extra soil. Don't allow this planting to dry out and keep soil evenly moist, but not saturated, with water.

Camellias bloom best with acidic soil. Before placing camellias in the planter, put a teaspoon of used coffee grinds or a teaspoon of Espoma Hollytone® under each camellia rootball.

PLANT OPTIONS

When purchasing the camellias, if the 'Spring's Promise' variety is not available, check to see that the camellia you are buying is hardy to zone 6. Several other cultivars of camellia that could be substituted for it are 'Yuletide', 'April Remembered', and 'Winter's Star'.

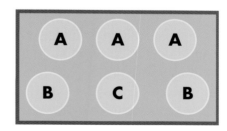

Spruced Up For Winter

SUN PREFERENCE	CONTAINER SIZE	DIFFICULTY LEVEL
Full Sun	Extra Large	Easy

Shopping List

- Container mix potting soil
- 1 5-gallon-sized blue spruce (*Picea pungens glauca* 'Fat Albert') **A**
- 3 2-gallon-sized nandinas (*Nandina domestica* 'Wood's Dwarf') **B**
- 3 1-gallon-sized sedums (*Sedum* 'Angelina') **C**
- 9 pansies (*Viola* x *wittrockiana* Matrix® 'Rose Wing') **D**

Wintertime plantings are a wonderful way to experiment with foliage and texture in your containers. A container recipe like this one becomes more than just a show of color—it works almost as a piece of art with structure and form that can accent your landscape or outdoor sitting area. The nandina's soft oval leaves contrast nicely with the stiff spruce branches. The sedums, with their thick chartreuse leaves, mimic the spruce needles, and take on a rosy tone in cooler weather that is reflected in the pansies and changing hues of the nandinas. Happy, round pansy faces randomly pop up through the nandinas giving the container planting an ever-changing display. If it's placed near an electrical outlet, it can be decorated for the holidays with tiny white lights or even with weather-tolerant decorations.

To assemble this container, place enough container mix potting soil in the planter so that the spruce can be centered and positioned so that the top of the rootball is lower than the container's rim. Add more soil around the rootball, filling the container to about 6 inches below the rim of the planter. Plant the nandinas and sedums next, adding more soil if needed. Slightly tilt these plants toward the rim of the container to enhance the "spilling over" look. Lastly, place the pansies as shown by the planting diagram.

The 'Fat Albert' blue spruce and nandinas are slow growing and need little to no pruning, so they could easily live in this planter for several years as long as they are maintained properly. This planting is very low maintenance, needing watering only when the top two inches of soil are dry to the touch. Fertilize with a general-purpose fertilizer in early spring and midsummer if it's left year-round in the planter. Replace pansies in spring with calibrachoas. A spruce is happier in cooler climates so make sure this planting gets some protection from the hot afternoon sun if you live south of the Mason-Dixon line and are maintaining this planting year-round.

PLANT OPTIONS

'Golden Sword' yucca or Gold Coast® juniper (Juniperus x pfitzeriana 'Aurea Improved') could be substituted for the nandina in climates colder than zone 6. Icee Blue® Yellow Wood (Podocarpus elongatus 'Monmal') works as an alternative to the spruce for those with winters warmer than zone 8.

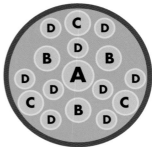

Wild Winter Window Box

SUN PREFERENCE	CONTAINER SIZE	DIFFICULTY LEVEL
Full Sun	Large	Moderate

Shopping List

- 44-inch-length iron hayrack with coco-liner
- Brackets (for hanging the hayrack on a balcony railing or fence)
- Container mix potting soil
- 2 1-gallon-sized dwarf golden arborvitaes (*Thuja orientalis* 'Aurea Nana') **A**
- 3 1-gallon-sized yuccas (*Yucca filamentosa* 'Bright Edge') **B**
- 8 yellow violas (*Viola* x *wittrockiana*) **C**
- 5 rose pansies (*Viola* x *wittrockiana*) **D**
- 6 violas (*Viola* x *wittrockiana* 'True Blue') **E**
- 5 purple wintercreepers (*Euonymus fortunei* 'Coloratus') **F**

Why let a window be the only place you think about hanging a hayrack planter! Whether you hang this recipe off a balcony, under a window, or along a fence as pictured here, this is a colorful option for winter planting. Hayrack planters are notorious for drying out quickly with their permeable coco-liners so choose drought-tolerant plants as shown here. You can also line the planters with a plastic trash bag that has 5 or 6 half-inch-sized holes poked through it for drainage. But line along the bottom inside of the coco-liner before adding soil, poke holes through the plastic only, and then add soil (this is the voice of experience talking).

When planting these hayrack planters, I find it easier to fill the planter with potting mix only halfway and the position the yuccas and arborvitaes where they are evenly spaced along the planter. Then I add remaining soil to within 1 inch from top of the coco-liner. Place remain plantings as shown in the diagram.

The purple wintercreepers, if they're planted before cooler weather has settled in, will be green until they get hit with a few nights of winter temperatures. Wintercreeper takes on this rich purplish red hue throughout the colder season, adding to the color drama of this combination. Sometimes you will find the 'Bright Edge' yucca sold by its common name of variegated Adam's needle. Water only when soil is dry to the touch.

PLANT OPTIONS

Another yucca that gives a vibrant gold winter color is 'Color Guard', which can be substituted for the 'Bright Edge' yucca. Both of these yucca plants produce a fragrant and long-lasting flower stalk in the spring.

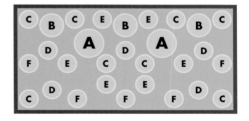

Winter Party

SUN PREFERENCE	CONTAINER SIZE	DIFFICULTY LEVEL
Full Sun	Large	Easy

Shopping List

- Container mix potting soil
- 3 1-gallon-sized variegated English hollies (*Ilex aquifolium*) **A**
- 3 1-gallon-sized cotoneasters (*Cotoneaster dammeri* 'Coral Beauty') **B**
- 3 sedums (*Sedum reflexum* 'Angelina') **C**

Winter plantings bring a richness of texture to your container gardens. In this recipe there are angular leaves of the hollies, the delicate oval leaves and round berries of the cotoneasters, and the soft, thick petals of sedums. Transitions of color keep this combination interesting throughout winter as the chartreuse sedums deepen to a bronze tone and the green cotoneaster leaves take on a purple tinge as the temperatures go down. Place your planter in a full sun spot to enjoy the best transition of color. While these plants can handle a partial sun location, you may not get as much color intensity as you would in a full sun location.

The sedums, cotoneasters, and hollies are all easy to care for. All three of these plants require you to water throughout the winter only when soil becomes dry to the touch, which can be one to three times a week. The recipe is designed to give color and interest for winter plantings but it can be left in the planter year-round if you like.

Remember to fertilize this planting in late winter and early summer with a product like Espoma's Holly-tone® or a 10-10-10 slow-release fertilizer. After several years of growing in a planter, these shrubs will need to be transplanted to a larger container, or you can transition them into the ground in your landscape.

When planning your winter containers, think about landscaping projects that you may have on the agenda for a future date. If a few of the larger *Ilex aquifolium* and cotoneasters are needed for the project, save a little money by purchasing these one-gallon-sized plants and let them grow for a year or two as this container recipe. By the time they have outgrown the container they are ready for the landscape.

Enjoy these plants indoors at your next party by snipping off little branches of the hollies or cotoneasters to dress up your napkin rings or to add to a flower arrangement. It's very charming.

PLANT OPTIONS

This type of variegated holly is winter hardy to zone 6 only, so those in colder climates will want to substitute Euonymous fortunei *'Emerald 'N Gold' for the* Ilex aquifolium.

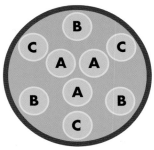

Thrillers, Fillers, and Spillers: Designing Your Own Container

Let's say that you've grown a few containers on your own, you've gotten a little confidence to try something new, and you're ready to design your own container. Here are a few design tips to keep in mind that will help you on your way. One of the phrases that is often heard in container planting is that a container needs to have "a thriller, a filler, and a spiller." Three plant growth habits help to make up this design.

A **thriller** is a vertical or upright plant, which gives a planter height. It is sometimes the "centerpiece" of the container recipe. A few examples of plants that are often used as thrillers are:

- Dracaena palm (*Cordyline*)
- Tropical hibiscus (*Hibiscus rosa-sinensis*)
- Mandevilla vine (on a trellis)
- Grasses such as *Pennisetum* 'Rubrum'
- 'Sky Pencil' holly (*Ilex crenata*)
- Camellia

A **filler** is a mounding plant whose stems have more of a bushy and arching form. A filler plant will "fill in" the area around the taller plant, should be shorter in height during the season's growing period than the "thriller," and looks best if the foliage is significantly different the other plants in the container. A few filler plant examples are:

- Ferns
- Coral bells
- Euphorbia
- Lantana
- Loropetalum
- Caladium
- Ornamental peppers

The **spiller** plants are trailing plants that flow over the edge of the container. Examples of spiller plants are:

- Sweet potato vine (*Ipomoea batatas*)
- Ivy geranium (*Pelargonium peltatum*)
- Creeping jenny (*Lysimachia*)
- Torenia
- Vinca vine
- Ivy (*Hedera helix*)
- Candytuft (*Iberis*)

Sometimes you may opt for using just two of these elements such as the filler and spiller for containers like window boxes, or a thriller and spiller when dramatic impact is desired.

Foliage & Color

Look at the foliage of the plants you are using and combine large oval leaves with narrow blades of grass, frilly foliage with glossy oval leaves, heavy foliage with light, delicate foliage. When it comes to foliage shape, contrast is the goal you are trying to achieve. Conversely, look for color that is echoed or repeated in the other plants in your recipe. For instance, a plant with purple foliage can be paired with a plant whose flower may be yellow but which has a purple throat. Combining several plants that echo one another's color gives the planting continuity while the foliage/textural contrasts make the planting more interesting.

Plant Like With Like

Remember to combine plants that like the same type of environment; that is, all are either shade loving, part-sun loving, or sun loving, and which like the same type of soil moisture requirements.

Now, Have Fun

There! You've got the basics of container planting design. Now, go out there and have some fun!

Containerscaping

When Joni Mitchell released her song "Big Yellow Taxi" in the late 1970s she sang, "They paved paradise, and put up a parking lot." People all over the world were nodding their heads in agreement at the dire concern that trees would be removed, placed in museums, and the world would be covered with concrete.

"We're doomed!"

"All is lost!"

Goodness gracious, folks needed to stop their bellyaching and talk to die-hard gardeners. They would find out that a world paved with concrete does not slow a plant lover down much at all. Don't take me wrong—I love the fact that natural areas and native plants are becoming a high priority in community developments. But not everyone has the luxury of rich soil and open areas to landscape, so utilizing container gardening has become a popular option from the balcony bound to those who just don't want to deal with the hard, packed clay soil in their backyard.

Containerscaping can be used to create an entire landscape. Most often, though, the use of containers is more supplementary to overall landscape design. Container plantings can be used to define an area, creating an intimate garden room in the landscape or outlining the sitting area of an outdoor café. Rectangular planters are a good choice for creating a distinct border. (I caution you to use large planters, not less than 18 inches high, otherwise you risk having a border that then can become a tripping hazard to the easily distracted.)

Container gardeners can also be used as privacy shield. If you like to entertain, but don't want everyone walking past your balcony to have a clear view of the great party you're having, use planters hanging from your balcony railing stocked with tall angelonia or coleus and cascades of petunias or mandevillas to obscure their line of sight. The sight of floriferous containers can be more eye-catching than gabbing, lipsticked guests. Planters filled with evergreens, a Japanese maple, or those lemon trees that you bring indoors every year also serve as lovely screening on a porch or patio, without being too obvious that you really don't want everyone seeing you drink your morning coffee. Even window boxes planted with tall annuals can screen the view inside when you want to open the windows to enjoy the evening air.

Empty walls alongside driveways or sidewalks can be an eyesore, but can be easily remedied by incorporating iron wall planters or a cluster of tall glazed planters billowing with 'Kimberly Queen' ferns or upright *Cordyline*. Hang hayrack planters filled with color or foliage plants along an empty fence that you see through the window every time you sit in your favorite living room chair. I've used containerscaping to dress up townhomes with tiny patio courtyards as a way to hide air-conditioning units or electrical boxes.

Container plantings are a creative way to bring interest and color into the blank spaces of the winter landscape. Rather than just plant a bed of pansies and kale for fall and winter, add a container to bring height and structure into the design. Containerscaping also allows you to keep tropical plantings as a "permanent" part of your landscape. Let's say you really want a large standard bougainvillea as a part of your landscape design, but you know that this involves purchasing a new one every year because it's not winter hardy. Place a container where you want the tree to be located, find a plastic or pressed fiber pot that will fit inside that container, and plant your bougainvillea in that pot. Enjoy your container throughout the spring, summer, and early fall, then bring the inner pot indoors for the winter. Fill the empty container that you left outdoors with another insert (plastic or pressed fiber pot) filled with pansies or maybe a live dwarf Alberta spruce that you'll decorate for the holidays, or fill it with decorative cut branches of winterberry, red-twig dogwood, magnolia, hollies, or junipers.

Enhance your landscape by placing pots of edibles on the empty spots in your yard filled with mint (make sure you trim it as it spills over and before it reaches the ground!), bush beans, tomatoes, blueberries, strawberries, or just about any other edible you want to try. You can save a little on landscaping cost by using container plantings to elevate a young, slow-growing tree or shrub that might get missed in the landscape. Once it has reached a more visible height, you can then plant it in the ground. Window boxes and containers also help to bring the eye up to draw attention to decorative shutters or ironwork, to guide the eye down a pathway, or to create structural diversity in a parterre garden or in a vista of monoculture plantings. Use containers to introduce plants into your landscape that would not naturally co-exist with the surrounding plants such as creating a water garden in the midst of drought-loving sedums and evergreens. A few things need to be remembered when you're containerscaping:

- Always use good quality container mix that is porous (well draining).

- Make sure that water can easily be accessed (and don't forget using tubing).

- For year-round planters, use good quality containers that are cast stone, metal, thick plastic, or fiberglass. I have used glazed clay planters in my zone 6 area, but I always use an insert (a plastic pot or pressed fiber pot) that I plant and then drop into my container.

- Always raise containers up off the ground by at least one inch. Pot feet come in a whole host of options—the idea is to prevent any water draining through the pot's drainage hole from freezing the container to the ground.

- Fertilize! Plants in containers usually require more water than plants in the ground, which means that nutrients are being washed out. Learn the fertilizing requirements for the plants in your container and faithfully apply. A weekly feeding of compost tea is also helpful.

Container plantings are often an afterthought and are used to spruce up lackluster gardens for a special event. Containerscaping, however, should be a component in landscape design, with irrigation and planter design determined in the planning process. Even for those renting a home or apartment, container plantings can help make a temporary location feel more personalized and provides the opportunity to begin collecting unique or memorable plants.

"Don't it always seem to go, that you don't know what you've got till it's gone."

You can create a lush containerscape, maybe even a paved paradise, when you fill it with potted gardens.

PARTY READY:
HOLIDAY AND SEASONAL CONTAINER IDEAS

Creating holiday or seasonal planter designs is a little like selecting an outfit's accessories for a night out on the town; one person's fun, colorful look can appear to other folks like a gaudy showgirl. Most of the time, holiday planters can be created simply by taking what you already have planted and making it holiday ready. I have a friend who plants a red twig dogwood, black mondo grass, and yellow pansies in her containers every fall. During the Christmas holidays, all she does is place a white iron dove amongst the red twig dogwood branches, making a very simple, yet poignant, holiday planter.

Many of the ideas shared here will be ones that you'll just slap your head and say, "I could have thought of that," so consider them just a little something to jiggle your thought processes. One of the easiest and least expensive ways to create holiday planters is to look around to see what is either in your garden or your attic that you can use as decoration. One November, my neighbor had just given his Foster holly, which was thick with berries, a severe pruning, and he had piled the branches on the street for the city

to pick up. He was more than happy for me to take as many branches as I wanted—these branches soon became the centerpieces of my holiday planters. I used a mixture of glossy magnolia leaves, some longleaf pine branches, and other evergreens such as false cypress (*Chamaecyparis*) and spruce to fill in around the planter. You can use other natural products like yellow or red twig dogwood branches, boxwood cuttings, nandina branches or berries, lichen-covered branches, juniper branches, and any interesting branches loaded with pinecones or berries. Always remember to ask permission from neighbors or public places before cutting any live branches.

A great fall look is easy to accomplish by mixing ornamental pepper plants, crotons, and orange or yellow mums. And don't forget adding branches of colorful fall leaves! A bonus—after you are done using them, they can go in your compost pile. Also in the fall, plant a container with a layer of spring-blooming bulbs and cover them with a layer of pansies or violas for a great spring show. Miniature blooming azaleas and hydrangeas underplanted with *Bacopa* or *Fuschia* will produce a wonderful fresh spring look. If you like, add brightly colored Easter eggs to the planter to celebrate the Easter season.

I like to leave the container mix potting soil from summer or autumn planters in my containers so that I can stick any branches into the potting mix to help hold them in position. This also allows you to maintain a little moisture in the branches if you water the display once a week or so (unless you are in freezing conditions). An assortment of three to four evergreens with a berry branch is usually all you need to design an attractive planter. Depending on the season, adding a large red, orange, or gold bow around the top of the planter, or hanging a few brightly colored Christmas balls, or setting small pumpkins or gourds around the base of the branches adds a festive touch. You can also spray paint pinecones or dried hydrangea blossoms with gold to insert among the branches.

Your choices are virtually limitless as you can use decorative objects in and around your containers to be party ready—anytime of the year!

USDA Hardiness Zones Map

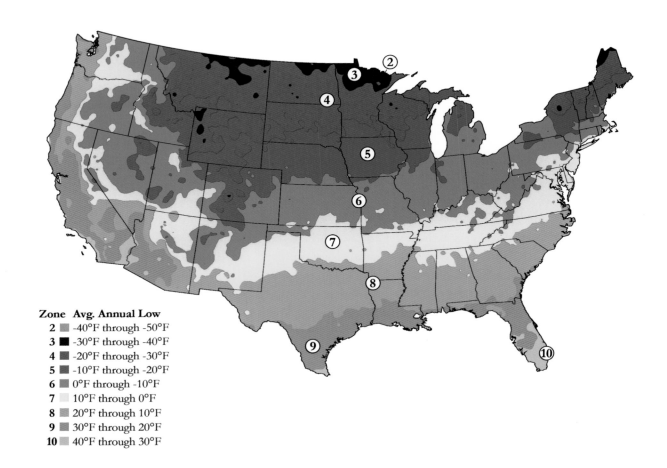

Zone	Avg. Annual Low
2	-40°F through -50°F
3	-30°F through -40°F
4	-20°F through -30°F
5	-10°F through -20°F
6	0°F through -10°F
7	10°F through 0°F
8	20°F through 10°F
9	30°F through 20°F
10	40°F through 30°F

source: http://www.arborday.org/media/map_change.cfm

Differences between 1990 USDA Hardiness Zones and 2006 arborday.org Hardiness Zones Reflect Warmer Climate

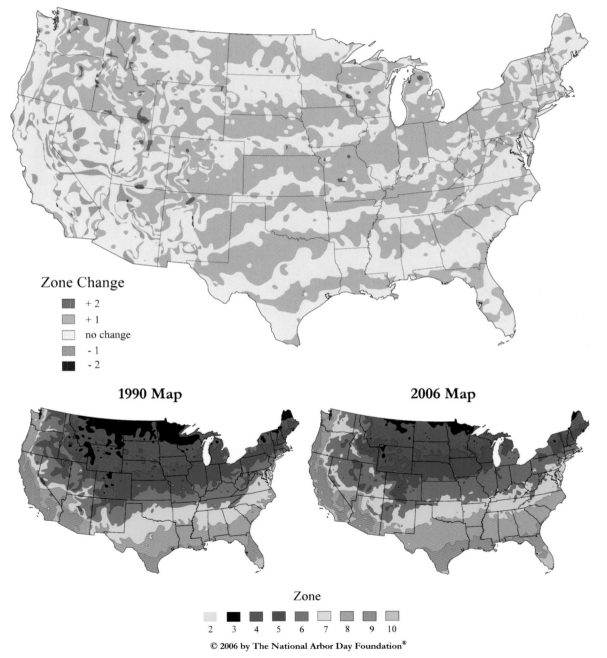

Zone Change

- +2
- +1
- no change
- -1
- -2

1990 Map   2006 Map

Zone

2 3 4 5 6 7 8 9 10

© 2006 by The National Arbor Day Foundation®

SOURCES

You can find many great products at your local home-improvement stores, at garden centers, and on the Internet. These are just a few of the companies and sources that I have used over the years. Check these Websites to purchase planters or to find a garden center or store near you that carries their products.

Containers

When it comes to containers, I'm a strong believer that you get what you pay for. Good quality containers will last years and they are worth the investment. Here are several companies that carry many of the planters that I have used over the years, several of which are shown throughout this book. Cast stone planters (many are offered from Campania International) become more interesting with age. Both cast stone planters and polyethylene planters are good types for year-round planting.

- Campania International, Inc.: www.campaniainternational.com
- Flower Framers™: www.flowerframers.com
- Haddonstone: www.haddonstone.com
- Hooks & Lattice: www.hooksandlattice.com
- Jackson Pottery Inc.: www.jacksonpottery.com
- Longshadow: www.longshadow.com
- Riverside Plastics: www.riverside-plastics.com

Plants

Your best sources for locating the plants for your container recipes are your local home-improvement and garden centers. But, one of the best-kept secrets in many areas is the state university trial or test gardens. Check with your local agricultural Extension Service office to find out if your state university has gardens that you can visit and see, first-hand, those plants that are growing well in *your* area. Many local botanical gardens will have container gardens and trial garden sections that are tagged with plant varieties so you can see how these plants handle the conditions in your zone. But if you want to learn more about the plants mentioned in these recipes, want to order a particular plant, or want to find out about certain varieties that could be substituted, check out these Websites.

- All-America Selections (AAS): www.all-americaselections.org
- Annie's Annuals and Perennials: www.anniesannuals.com
- Ball Horticultural Company: www.ballhort.com
- Barbara Wise: www.bwisegarden.blogspot.com
- Bluestone Perennials, Inc.: www.bluestoneperennials.com
- Brent and Becky's Bulbs: www.brentandbeckysbulbs.com
- Garden Debut®: www.gardendebut.com
- Monrovia: www.monrovia.com
- Plant Delights Nursery, Inc.: www.plantdelights.com
- Proven Winners®: www.provenwinners.com
- Simply Beautiful®: www.simplybeautifulgardens.com
- The Trial Gardens at UGA: www.ugatrial.hort.uga.edu
- White Flower Farm: www.whiteflowerfarm.com

Container Mix Potting Soil

Yes, what's on the inside really *does* make a difference. Potting mix should contain a mixture of peat moss, pine bark, and either vermiculite or perlite, plus some type of slow-release fertilizer or starter fertilizer. Some options that I've been happy with are Fafard's Complete Container Mix, Monrovia Organics Potting Soil, and Miracle-Gro Moisture Control Potting Mix.

Garden Tools

Having a few essential garden tools can make your planting process a whole lot easier. I've mentioned several times in the recipes about using a hori-hori knife; that's a multipurpose hand tool that is at the top of my gardening tool essential category. A good-quality hand-pruner, a trug tub (a light-weight, flexible polyethylene carrier), and work gloves are items that I also keep with me when I'm either planting or maintaining containers. Most of these items can be found at your local home-improvement and garden centers, but you can also find them through the following sources.

- A.M. Leonard: www.amleo.com
- Corona: www.coronatoolsusa.com
- Gardener's Supply Company: www.gardeners.com (the hori-hori knife sold here is called a "Multi-purpose Garden Knife")
- Kinsman Company: www.kinsmangarden.com
- The Home Depot: www.homedepot.com
- Lowe's: www.lowes.com
- Target: www.target.com

Barbara Wise,
In Her Own Words

Early in my horticultural career I was scheduled to meet a potential landscaping client at her home to evaluate her needs. Walking up to the stately home, I expected to be greeted by a tuxedo-clad butler or matronly housekeeper. The melee that spilled out the door washed away my misguided expectations and gave me my first clue to the horticultural needs of this newest budding gardener. After our greetings, the mother, still in her PJs with a baby on one hip, two toddlers at her feet, and a golden retriever circling the crowd, announced her wishes, "I want a lot of flowers but I'm on a tight budget, and everything I plant seems to die." The gauntlet had been thrown down and the challenge began. How could I provide this client with plantings that would make her feel successful and love to garden?

Although I had a degree in Family Resource Management from Auburn University, my fascination with the design side of the plant world (and I am admittedly more drawn to the landscaping side of horticulture than the edible side) led me to transform my gardening hobby into a horticulture career. As a lifelong songwriter, I thought that living in Nashville would be a way to finally get my songwriting career to take off. What I found, however, was that folks were more interested in what I had composed in my containers and garden than hearing any song I'd composed!

The more I learned about growing things, the more I wanted to learn. After getting my brood of four boys in school, I went to work at a local garden center to gain experience in greenhouse growing and plant knowledge. I figuratively sat at the feet of horticultural experts Rita Randolph and Linda Askey to glean their knowledge of the unique needs for container gardening. After completing a Master Gardener course, I started working for a development company in their horticulture department. As the Director of Garden Installation for Southern Land Company, I get to oversee the planting of hundreds of annual beds and containers each year, work within the communities with our homeowners teaching classes on gardening, write for several gardening magazines, have a monthly gardening column in *Nashville House & Home & Garden*, and write a gardening blog. I was even privileged to create a backyard redo for the Discovery Channel television show *Picture This* for country music star Heidi Newfield.

Here's a little bit of history. My Momma, Daddy, and both sets of grandparents were the sowers of my plant passions. Mable Hutchison, my maternal grandmother, or Hutchie as we called her, was widowed in her late 30s and never remarried. She taught English in high school until she retired in her 70s, was involved in her church, and she gardened. I remember summers of dividing daylilies in the one-half-acre field next to her white clapboard home and replanting hundreds of irises that she'd dug up to share or move, of gathering scuppernongs and sucking the juice out until my cheeks ached and belly bulged, of shucking corn and shelling peas with Hutchie and Aunt Blanche while Uncle Jones plowed those red clay fields, of spending late nights canning veggies from the garden because the days were too hot in a Southern home with no air conditioning. Hutchie never blogged or even wrote about her gardening; it was just part of maintaining life. But she loved that part of life and taught me to love it too.

Momma carried on her love for gardening. In the picture above, Momma is pregnant with me and picking fruit off one of the many apple, peach, or pear trees around Hutchie's house. On the farm where I grew up, there was always corn during the summer to be picked on Sunday after church for lunch, okra to be fried, and a cow to be milked.

My Aunt Julie Tinkey taught me a whole different side of the horticulture world. Her gardens were a story to be told. As we wandered about the acres surrounding her home, I learned there was a message or meaning connected to each plant. A garden for Aunt Julia was a place for discovering oneself and learning truth. Meandering paths, boulders from the old homeplace, rambling roses, plants shared from friend to friend—gardening was an artwork painted to reflect life. I learned through my aunt to see the landscape as a palette to create those dreams that warm our nights and refresh our days.

Daddy was a forester. He and Daddy George started a timber company called Georgia Timberlands. Daddy taught me to love what he called "the cathedral of the pines." He was immensely careful to teach me to understand that the business of timber management was to treasure the land and leave it more ecologically valuable than when you found it. Daddy was a tree hugger before tree huggers became the "In" thing to be.

Growing up, I remember camellia bushes blooming under my open windows in winter and the wisteria throughout the trees that scented my summer nights. But what seemed to have had the most profound effect on me were the window boxes! Behind Daddy, Momma, Grandma Peake, and Daddy George in the photo on the facing page is one of the large, deep window boxes that underlined each outward vista from my mid-Georgia childhood home, each one full and overflowing for three seasons.

For the last several years I've spent many hours planting thousands of window boxes and have felt like I was the luckiest woman on earth to have this job. Suddenly it all started to make sense. Subconsciously, with each window box, I was recreating a little of the rich horticultural history that has guided and enriched my life; just maybe I was creating a new memory for some child who would look out their window to see life waiting to be discovered.

What I found that I really love to do, however, is help other people be successful in their gardens—finding the right plant for the right place for the right people. Helping that client who says, "I want a lot of flowers but I'm on a tight budget, and everything I plant seems to die," became my driving force when designing container plantings and garden beds. What I found by gardening in my own yard was that sometimes just learning a few little tricks of the trade saved me time and money down the road. I now have eight large garden beds and around twenty-four containers in my one acre lot; most of those beds and container plantings are "experiment stations" for trying out the latest plants to hit the market or testing a new type of soil or gardening product. Working in my own yard after working all day at the company greenhouse or within the company's developments means that sometimes I'm planting bulbs by a headlamp and that the plants I'm trying out are *not* overly pampered.

Planting has become not just a profession for me, but a true passion. I hope it becomes your passion too.

—*Barbara*

Publisher's Note: Barbara Wise lives and gardens in Brentwood, Tennessee, with her husband and youngest son. This is her first book.

INDEX